woven
treasures

········

one-of-a-kind bags
with folk weaving techniques

········

sara
lamb

INTERWEAVE.
interweavestore.com

dedication: To my always supportive Mother

acknowledgments:

To my editor, Anne, for initiating and shepherding me through this book process
To the weavers from whom I have learned so much
To my friends for their advice, ideas and encouragement
To my two sons, who so often woke up and went to sleep to the whir of the wheel
    and the beat of the loom
and to my husband, Kurt, for his love and support.

Editor: Anne Merrow
Technical Editor: David L. Johnson
Illustrator: Gayle Ford
Photography: Joe Coca
Technical Photography and Photo Stylist: Ann Sabin Swanson
Designer: Lee Calderon
Production: Katherine Jackson

Interweave Press LLC
201 East Fourth Street
Loveland, CO 80537 USA
interweavestore.com

Printed in China by
Asia Pacific Offset Ltd.

10 9 8 7 6 5 4 3 2 1

Library of Congress
Cataloging-in-Publication Data

Lamb, Sara, 1951-
Woven Treasures : one-of-a-kind
bags with folk weaving techniques
/ Sara Lamb.
    p. cm.
Includes bibliographical references
and index.
 ISBN 978-1-59668-102-6
1. Hand weaving. I. Title.
TT848.L323 2009

contents

weaving the story

········

I have been a weaver for over thirty years. I began floor-loom weaving by exploring fabric structures, like twills, rosepath, and overshot, then invested in a more complex loom so I could try structures on eight shafts.

After a few years, I took a class on weaving cotton fabrics, focusing on color and fiber choice rather than complexity of structure. It was great fun to weave lengths of plain fabric, useful fabric, fabric which had a wonderful drape and hand, using fine wefts. I blended colors, I dyed yarns, I learned to dye using complex techniques like ikat and painted warps. I wove lengths and lengths and made them up into garments. I don't enjoy sewing much, so I concentrated on a simple timeless kimono-based garment that fit me, set off the fabrics nicely, and was quick and easy to sew.

My closet, full of colorful woven clothes.

At some point, though, I had enough clothing, so I wove hand towels, scarves, and shawls for a while. One day I had a length of silk left over from a scarf that was too short to be another scarf but too good to throw away. I decided to make a bag. I needed to learn a few new tricks to weave the bands and how to embellish the bag.

I had more leftover fabrics, and I made more bags. Through trial and error (and classes in bead and wire techniques), I learned what I wanted to know. Soon I was weaving cloth specifically for the bags rather than using leftovers. Each idea spawned others, and a whole series of bags grew out of that one piece of leftover silk. I made bags based on puns, bags based on ideas, bags honoring women in history, legend, and myth. (For more on my bag series, see page 138.) I wove beads into bags, and my frustration with not finding colors I wanted in beads led me to explore knotted pile.

This book is the result of the study of ancient weaving techniques. There is a relaxing and repetitive nature to the process, and the textiles you can create with them are durable, utilitarian, and endlessly fascinating.

The projects in this book teach, one by one, the techniques that I learned in order to make the bags I wanted to weave. These are the timeless weaving techniques—knotting, wrapping, and twisting the weft—that I have come to use and enjoy. It is my hope that these projects will make weaving come alive for you and inspire further exploration of weaving. The looms are simple and fun to use, give excellent results, and are very flexible.

In planning the projects for this book, I kept several things in mind: I wanted the bags to be useful, emulating the cultures that inspired them and that still weave these techniques. I wanted the projects to increase in complexity, adding techniques or subtleties with each project. I wanted them to be simple to construct, and I wanted them to be beautiful. All of the projects are based on a plain-weave structure, the simple over-and-under weaving that is familiar to most people as cloth. The use of supplemental wefts in the textile construction (as in cut pile) makes the surface more complex but does not change the underlying plain-weave structure.

Because the rigid-heddle loom was new to me, I started (as you will) with a simple bag with the cloth woven on one heddle and band woven on two. I made several versions of the bag so that I could learn how to set up the loom, how it operates, and plan the subsequent projects. Each subsequent project includes a new technique, so you might wish to make the projects in consecutive order, learning a new technique or variation with each bag as you go.

In the final chapter, I present some tips and techniques to help you create projects that reflect your design ideas, so that your weaving is a reflection not only of the wonderful techniques presented here, but is also your own personal expression.

slow cloth

Weaving has been a human activity since before recorded history. Textile production was once the most labor-intensive of all human endeavors, requiring more human power to produce than any other basic necessity. Everyone could participate, from small children to the elderly, and people understood the process from fiber to fabric to finished goods.

With the industrial revolution, every aspect of textile production has become further and further removed from the eyes and knowledge of people in their daily world. Machines now perform the tasks that were once common activities, from preparing fibers, spinning, dyeing, to weaving and even sewing.

Today, textile production is no longer common, and there is a mystery about the process. Most people rarely give a thought to the amount and variety of textiles in their lives, where the fibers come from, by whom and how the fabrics are made. Many people are under the impression that even handweaving is only accomplished on complex looms that take much study to master. Yet most handweaving in the world is still done on simple looms made with sticks and string, relying on the skill of the weaver rather than the complexity of the tools to create the fabric. While simple, such weaving is by no means limited in scope. The surprise is that so few techniques and such simple tools can be used to create such a variety of textiles.

These techniques are worked at a different pace than life today—slower, more deliberate, and more contemplative. Some of the things I admire most about village and tribal textiles are the anomalies showing the hand of the maker in unusual and charming ways. Machines can make cloth with a perfection and complexity that shows no sign of its human maker. Weaving by hand is not all about perfection. It is about craftsmanship, personal expression, beauty, and utility.

When we discuss any craft, there is often mentioned the question of

time. How much time did this take to make? How long will it take you to finish this? If you are selling handmade goods, what is your time worth? These projects are not necessarily fast to make; it is not like weaving yards of fabric where you can bang out a length every day. The time frame for completing these bags is more like knitting, cross-stitch or needlepoint: a few weeks, a month, a period of time. I think of it more in terms of rows per night, so that if a project has thirty-five rows, and I get five rows done every evening, it will take me a week to make. There are a few more evenings for the band, and then everything needs to be washed, pressed, and sewn to shape. So time passes. In that time you are making something to keep, to use, to give; something that is durable, and something that is timeless, despite the time it takes to make.

looms, tools,
and yarns

You don't need to be an expert weaver to make any of the projects in this book, and you don't need a lot of complicated gear either. If you have a multi-shaft loom and specialized weaving equipment, you can use them for any of these projects, but they can be made using very simple tools—just as the weavers who developed the techniques did.

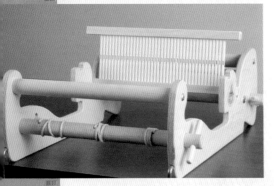

Above: A Schacht Flip in Stand
Below: A Schacht Cricket loom

looms

All of the bags in this book were woven on a rigid-heddle loom. This type of loom is readily available, accessible, and affordable. It is easy to set up, understand, and use. It can make two sheds and hold tight warp tension, the basic requirements for the weave structures presented here. It is also quiet, portable, and lightweight, making it easy to move from room to room or use in a group setting without disrupting the conversation. It is useful as a frame for holding cards in cardweaving (or tablet weaving) and can be set up for simple inkle bands and bands made using pick-up weave structures. Using the rigid-heddle loom for projects that take more time, like soumak and pile, means I can leave my big loom free for other weaving.

Rigid heddles have been in use since very early times. Early examples used for band weaving and tape weaving can be seen in many museums in New England and Europe. I had never used a rigid-heddle loom before starting these projects. I have now used three: the Schacht 15" Flip loom, the Ashford 16" standard rigid-heddle loom, and the Schacht Cricket. All performed well for most of the projects presented here; the Flip and Ashford can accommodate two heddles, but the Cricket holds only one.

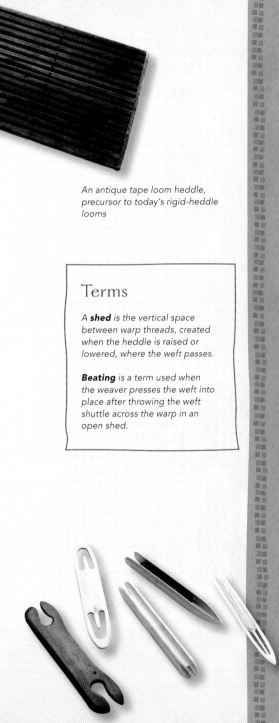

Many looms have an optional stand to hold the loom at a comfortable height for weaving fabric. I also weave some of the structures with the loom clamped on a worktable with a height of 37½" (95 cm), which allows me to stand and work at a comfortable height. When I weave knotted pile, I prop the loom on the counter and sit on a chair with a height of 18" (45.5 cm) to allow an almost vertical weaving surface.

A **heddle** is a device used to hold a warp thread and allow it to be manipulated (by hand or by the loom mechanism) to form the *shed* through which the weft will pass. Rigid heddles combine the function of two shafts, with slots for one set of warps and holes for another set of warps. The rigid heddle may also be used in place of a *beater* (see page 10).

Dent is the number of yarn spaces per inch; it determines how thick and how close the warp yarns can be. On a multishaft loom, there can be as many threads and heddles per inch as desired. On a rigid-heddle loom, the number of ends per inch is determined by the fixed heddles. To weave more ends per inch than there are spaces in the rigid heddle, you can use two heddles to weave twice as many ends per inch (see page 24).

An antique tape loom heddle, precursor to today's rigid-heddle looms

tools

Besides the loom, there are a few tools necessary for weaving the bags presented here.

Shuttles are used to carry the weft yarns during weaving. Rigid-heddle looms often come with a simple stick shuttle with points to keep the weft yarn in place. These work fine, but I prefer a netting shuttle or a belt shuttle with a few clever adaptations.

Terms

A **shed** is the vertical space between warp threads, created when the heddle is raised or lowered, where the weft passes.

Beating is a term used when the weaver presses the weft into place after throwing the weft shuttle across the warp in an open shed.

A **beater** is used to press the weft into place. For some projects, you can use the heddle to press the weft in place, but for firm cloth a separate beater may be needed.

Thread nippers are used for trimming yarns, especially knots in pile weaving. They are designed to hold comfortably inside the hand.

Machine embroidery scissors are useful for finish-trimming the surface of cut pile. My favorite pair are 6" offset Gingher machine embroidery scissors.

A **darning needle** is used to weave in weft ends and correct mistakes in weaving.

Several types of **tape measure** can be useful, including a retractable semi-rigid one for measuring the distance between pegs and a dressmaker's tape measure for measuring fabric.

A **sewing needle** and **thread** to match the project are needed to finish the bags.

A **sewing machine** with a zigzag function is used to finish the raw edges of fabric cut off the loom and in constructing the bags.

An **iron** and **ironing board** are used to attach interfacing as well as press out wrinkles.

yarns

I am a spinner and dyer, and I rely heavily on creating my own yarns for the projects that I weave. Nonetheless, I found several appropriate commercial yarns for every project that were readily available, inexpensive, and produced in a variety of colors. Yarns used for warp need to be smooth, durable, and inelastic, like the mercerized cotton used here. The weft yarns vary depending on the technique and use of the textile from smooth and firm to soft and fluffy.

There is no one right yarn for any of the techniques here, and the fiber, size, and amount of twist in your yarn choice will affect the hand and utility of the finished weaving.

fiber

I used three natural fibers for all of these projects: cotton, wool, and silk. These fibers are all renewable resources and have been cultivated for textile use since before recorded history.

cotton

Cotton is a plant-based cellulose used worldwide. Cotton fabrics can be soft, absorbent, easily laundered, and bleached for sanitary uses.

Cotton is relatively short fiber, with a length between ½" and 2" (1.3 and 5 cm). Its short staple means that the most durable yarn spun from cotton has lots of twist to hold the short fibers locked together as yarn. Cotton is moderately strong compared to other fibers and is strong when wet, making it easy to care for. It is relatively inelastic, so it wrinkles easily and does not return to shape when stretched. It can be damaged by excessive moisture, acid, and long exposure to sunlight.

The cotton yarns used here have been mercerized, a process that increases the strength of the fibers and makes them appear more lustrous. Mercerized cottons also accept dyes more readily, allowing for dark, intense colors.

Cotton is sold by yarn weight and the number of plies, and the numerical designations can be confusing. In the United States, the weight number of a cotton yarn is designated first,

Test all yarn colors for wash fastness. Wash a sample of the yarn as you would the final project: handwash in hot water, rinse, and lay flat to dry.

Terms

Wraps per inch *is a measure of a yarn's diameter.*

Grist *is the relationship between weight and length of a given yarn, usually expressed as yards per pound. Grist is the most accurate system for measuring yarn size because yarn density is included in the calculations.*

followed by the number of plies. Thus size 10 cotton of 2 plies would be written as 10/2.

The weight is determined by the number of 840-yard hanks that can be spun from a pound of fiber.

- If only one hank is spun, the yarn would be a very thick strand 840 yards long. The weight number associated with that yarn would be 1.

- Size 10 yarn means that ten 840-yard hanks would be spun from one pound of cotton, making that yarn 10 times finer than a size 1 yarn.

- If there is more than one strand in the yarn construction, the yarn number designates the number of plies. For example, size 1 yarn with 2 plies would be noted as 1/2.

The crochet cotton used in many of the projects is size 10, but it has 3 strands or plies and would be des-

ignated a 10/3 yarn. Crochet cotton is generally sold only by its weight number (in this case 10) and is presumed to have 3 plies. It is also very tightly twisted, often mercerized, and considered very durable.

The Tahki Cotton Classic used in several projects is generally sold for knitting, so there is no numbering system listed. The label lists yardage and weight, not yarn count. We can extrapolate a numerical count from the information given and a close look at the yarn. The yarn is a cabled construction, composed of 5 strands of 2-ply yarns re-plied together to form a cable with a surface that looks like rope. It has 988 yards per pound, a heavy yarn about the size of a 2/2 cotton, but with much more stability than a simple 2-ply yarn of the same weight.

wool

Longwool sheep produce a long-staple fiber suitable for hardwearing outer clothing, rugs, and bags. The most desirable characteristic of wool yarns used for these techniques is durability. The fibers and yarns are abraded during weaving, and the finished textile needs to withstand constant use.

There are several systems for classifying wool fibers, the most common of which is the worsted count system. Similar to cotton and spun silk counts, the first measurement refers to the number of 560-yard hanks that can be spun from a pound of wool. The second number refers to the number of singles that have been combined into a plied yarn.

Feel the yarns you are planning to use. You should find firm, smooth longwool fibers, luster, and a worsted-spun tightly twisted yarn. If the yarns are delicate or abrade easily, then they are best used for textiles where durability is not the key factor.

The projects in this book use cotton warps because even the wool yarns I use regularly as warps were too difficult to weave on the rigid-heddle loom. The heddle stretched the wool yarns too much when changing sheds. If you choose to use wool, look for well-spun, multiple-ply, tight-twist yarns that will withstand the abrasion during weaving. Look for wool that has been designated as spun for warp. Wool warps are durable and will slightly felt with finishing and use, making the textile very cohesive.

silk

Silk is a filament produced by silk worms as cocoons. The fibers are very fine in diameter, very strong, and lustrous. The fibers are a protein substance; they take dye readily in deep rich colors and are not damaged by acid process dyeing. Fine silk fibers are very durable, but they can be damaged by alkaline substances like chlorine bleach or perspiration and by sunlight. There are two types of silk normally used by weavers: reeled and spun.

Reeling is very labor and time intensive, as each cocoon must be unwound and the filament joined with other filaments to make a useable size thread. Several of these filaments

are reeled together, with a small amount of twist added to help hold the bundle together. After the reeling process, more twist may be inserted in a process called *throwing* (similar to spinning) and further twisted as two or more strands in a process called *doubling* (similar to plying). Spun silk uses the waste fibers from the reeling process. Spun silk does not have the strength of reeled silk, as it is composed of lengths of shorter fibers. Nor does it have the luster of reeled silk, as the many ends refract light and break up the smooth surface of the fiber. There are two common classifications for silk: bombyx (or cultivated) and tussah (also called "wild"). Bombyx silk is always bright white; tussah silks can be any degree of gold, tan, cinnamon, or brown.

Reeled silk is designated by a denier measurement, referring to the weight of the filament in a skein. A denier is equal to .05 grams. The count of a silk yarn is determined by the number of denier needed for a 450-yard skein.

It is the opposite of the cotton count system in that the higher the number, the heavier the yarn—low-denier silk is finer than high-denier silk.

Spun silk is measured by the same count as cotton: by the number of 840-yard hanks that can be spun from a pound of silk and the number of plies.

twist

The amount of twist inserted into a yarn is a factor in determining a yarn's suitability for various textile techniques. Warps need to be strong, but warps for knotted pile versus warps for fabrics need differing degrees of strength (i.e., twist).

Warps for the First Bag and Pick-up Tote are not very firmly beaten—a separate hand beater is not needed—so they can be less tightly twisted. The fabric will have a pliable hand and be softer to the touch. The weft-faced bags in plain weave, soumak, and knotted pile rely on a firm beat with a handheld beater. To stand up to this abrasion, the warp yarn needs to be strong, tightly twisted, and durable.

Weft yarns can have varying degrees of twist, depending on the end use of the intended fabric. Yarns used for pile weft need to be durable, but also need to bloom, or open up at the cut edge to create the velvet-like surface we associate with pile fabrics. Most wool yarns will do this when cut, and the projects use different yarns as pile, each creating a different surface appearance and hand.

substituting yarns

If you choose different yarns, evaluate your yarn choices based on the technique, the eventual use of the textile, and the properties of the yarn you choose. Does the yarn need to be durable? Does it need a long staple or will tight twist be able to overcome a short staple?

Though yardage per pound can help you find a good replacement yarn, there are other factors to consider; the amount of twist and yarn density will also affect the yarn's suitability. A woven sample is the only true test, but before committing to a sample, I use this quick method to test a seemingly comparable yarn. Take a short-length strand of any two yarns you wish to compare and twist them around each other to interlock them. If you run your fingers along the length of both yarns at the twist, you can feel whether the yarns are comparable grist.

Interlock two yarns and twist them. Run your fingers over the joint to feel whether they are compatible.

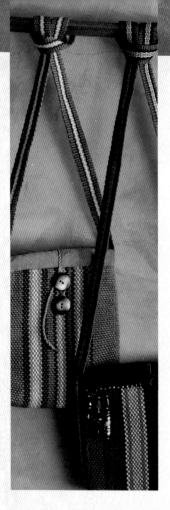

basic
weaving

········

The techniques required to make the projects in this book are very simple, but most of them will be unfamiliar even to experienced weavers of complex cloth. The only common weaving skills you will need to begin are warping, weaving a header, and plain weave. The directions in this chapter will teach you the necessary skills to begin weaving, which you can put into practice in the First Bag project on page 40.

I warped the projects in this book using the single peg system on a rigid-heddle loom, but they can be translated to a warping board, a table or floor loom, or a frame loom set up to weave with two sheds. Any loom you use for these projects needs to be able to create two sheds, hold a tight tension, and have a mechanism to advance the warp.

warp calculation worksheet

The projects in this book include directions for the width and length of the warp, but this formula is the basis for many weaving projects. It looks intimidating at first, but as you experiment and design your projects, you will understand the variables better.

- **Finished length (FL)** of the piece you wish to weave

- **Finished width (FW)** of the piece you wish to weave

- **Loom waste (W),** or the amount of yarn on the loom that can't be woven

- **Warping waste (WW),** or ends that are trimmed off as the warp is tied onto the loom

- **Weaving length take-up (T),** or the amount that the warp gets shorter going over and under the weft, in fabrics where this is applicable

- **Weaving width draw-in (D),** or the amount that the weaving narrows from the reed to the finished project

- **Shrinkage (S)** in both length and width, the amount that the finished piece gets smaller from finishing

- **Sett,** the number of strands of yarn in an inch (expressed in ends per inch, or epi)

FL + W + WW + T + S = length of yarn for warp

(FW + D + S) × sett (number of ends per inch) = number of ends in the warp

sett

We need to know what we want to weave in order to determine how to accomplish it. To set up the loom for weaving, we need to know the size and properties of the fabric we want to create. These bags vary in size, both length and width. We know the yarns we plan to use, so we can start from there.

To determine the *sett* of any yarn, wrap it loosely on a ruler or an inch gauge. The Tahki Cotton Classic yarn used in the First Bag measures 16 wraps per inch. If we sett the yarns at 16 ends per inch, no weft would show in the final fabric; it would be *warp faced. Balanced plain weave* is a fabric with an equal number of warps and wefts in the same area; divide the number of wraps of a yarn in half

Terms

Sett is the number of warp ends in a given width, usually per inch or centimeter.

Shots per inch refers to the number of weft passes (also called picks) in a given linear inch of fabric.

This yarn measures 16 wraps per inch.

to find the sett for a balanced plain weave. For a balanced plain weave in this yarn, use 8 ends per inch as the sett for the warps and weave 8 shots per inch in the weft, and the wefts should fill in the gaps created between the warps as you weave.

A wider sett will give a fabric where the weft dominates—there are more weft shots than warps in a given area. In weft-faced fabrics, the weft covers the warp entirely; no warp shows in the finished fabric. The fabric in the First Bags will be warp-dominant, with more *warp ends* than *weft picks* per square inch. The size of the weft for the band matters, too—it will determine how many shots per inch you can weave.

Warps and wefts shift in the weaving process and shrink in the finishing process, so any sett must be tested with a sample. A fabric is not finished until it is washed.

To make a firm fabric for the First Bag and Pick-up Tote, choose a sett that will be more warp dominant. Choose a number halfway between warp faced (16) and balanced plain weave (8), or 12 ends per inch. The weft will show and the weft size and color will matter, but the warp will be dominant in the fabric.

We need to know the finished size of the fabric we want to weave. For a bag that is 8" (20.5 cm) wide by 6" (15 cm) deep, with a 1" (2.5 cm) wide band (corresponding to a 1" [2.5 cm] wide bottom flap), we will need a fabric with the finished dimensions of 8" x 13" (20.5 x 33 cm). Multiply the sett (12 epi) by the width desired (8" [20.5 cm]) to find the number of ends needed (96).

There is also shrinkage (from finishing) and draw-in (the width of yarn pulled in by the weft) to consider when calculating for the width. To create a finished fabric with the exact dimensions, we could add some warp threads to our sample; in this case, the finished size is not critical, so we will leave it at 96 ends for our fabric. Next, we need to calculate the length of the warp. The finished fabric needs to be 13" (33 cm). There is also shrinkage and take-up to consider when calculating the length. Shrinkage and take-up allowance of 20% should be enough. I also like to add length to the warp for sampling different wefts (which includes cutting and washing a piece before the whole fabric is woven) to make sure my choices are correct.

We must also consider warping waste and loom waste when determining the length of the warp. Warping waste includes any length that is cut off in the process of warping, tying on, and weaving the header. Loom waste includes the length of warp that cannot be woven at the end of the warp; this varies from loom to loom. For the rigid heddles used in these projects, warping with the peg system, I allowed warping and loom waste of 18" (45.5 cm) each.

So to find the length of the warp needed, add:

- Finished length desired (FL): 13" (33 cm)
- Take-up (T) and shrinkage (S), an estimated 20%: 2.6" (6.5 cm)
- Warping waste (WW) and loom waste (W): 36" (91.5 cm)
- Plus room for sampling wefts (including cutting off a sample to wash before the entire length of fabric is woven): 8½" (21.5 cm)

With these factors in mind, I set up the loom with a 60" (152.5 cm) warp for all the projects. Because most of the warp yarns are inexpensive, I didn't mind cutting off the extra warp. I have a 60" (152.5 cm) table in my studio, so I clamped the loom to one end and the peg to the other and proceeded to warp the loom using the single-peg method (see page 21).

The bands required a longer warp of about 3 yards (3 meters).

(see page 21)

Terms

Take-up *refers to the warp that undulates over and under the weft during weaving. It varies with tension on the warp, weft choice, and sett.*

determining sett

The measurements of a yarn are useful as a starting point when determining suitability for a particular textile and how to sett the threads in the warp for any fabric you wish to weave. It also helps you determine which heddle to use.

The sett chart is a place to begin your exploration of a yarn's proper sett for the project you are working on. Samples will help determine if your calculations are accurate, and time and experience with a particular yarn also help. Using a fabric for its intended purpose is the only real test of proper sett.

The first two projects are sett close to make a sturdy fabric for durable bags. The First Bag is sett at 12 epi and the Pick-up Tote is sett at 20 epi in a plain weave, a close sett according to the chart above. The rest of the projects are weft-faced weaving. Since the weft on a weft-faced fabric must fit

between the warps easily, the weft grist and warp grist both determine the sett of the project. The weft yarn should easily pass between the warps but not leave excessive room on either side.

Experience and sampling help to determine the optimal sett, but there is always a range of possible setts, and you need to sample to determine how firm you want your finished fabric to be. Sampling is the best way to find the right sett for your project. Even if your fabric looks perfect on the loom, finishing will affect the hand of the fabric, so you can't really know the proper sett until you have woven and finished a sample. Warps relax when they are off the loom and finished, changing the number of wefts per inch. Measurements taken under tension always change as the threads are relaxed.

sett table

Yarn size	yd/lb	Suggested sett for plain weave
20/2 cotton	8,400	24–30
10/2 cotton	4,200	24–28
5/2 cotton	2,100	15–18
3/2 cotton	1,260	10–12
2/2 cotton	1,000	8–10
20/2 linen	3,000	20–24
12/1 linen	3,600	22–25
4/1 linen	1,400	12–15
20/2 worsted wool	5,600	20–24
12/3 worsted wool	2,160	15–18
6.5/1 wool	3,200	18–20
12/2 wool	3,000	18–20
7/2 wool	1,640	12–15
6.5/2 wool	1,600	10–12
1.3/1 wool	600	8–10
2.2/2 wool	550	8–10
22/2 cotton/linen blend	3,250	15–20

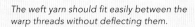

The weft yarn should fit easily between the warp threads without deflecting them.

single peg
warping method

Many looms come with a peg that can be clamped at a distance from the loom. Use the peg to measure and tie on the warp in one action.

single heddle

There are several ways to warp a loom; you may prefer to use the instructions that came with your loom. This technique is used for most of the projects.

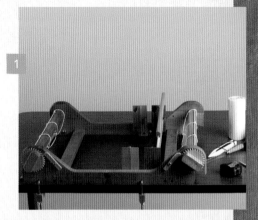

1. Set up the loom on a table or stand, securely clamped, and place the heddle in the neutral slot.

2. Secure the peg the intended distance (for the warp length) from the back apron bar.

3. Tie the first warp yarn to the back apron bar and thread (or sley) a loop through the leftmost slot of your warping plan with a threading hook. Take the warp loop around the peg and return to the back of the loom.

4. Take a second length of warp yarn around the warp bar, thread it through the next slot in sequence, and pull the loop through and around the peg.

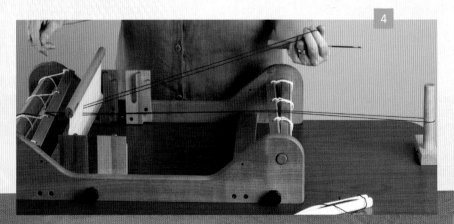

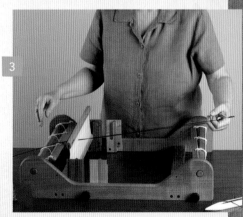

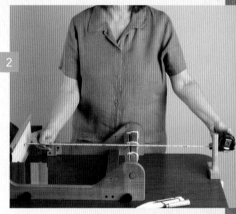

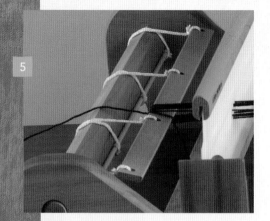

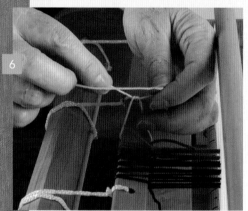

5 Note that the warp loop is pulled alternately from above and below the apron bar.

6 To change color, tie off the old warp and tie on a new color to the warp bar.

7 Repeat the process in color order according to your plan until all the slots you need are filled. Cut off the yarn at the source and tie the last tail to the warp bar.

8 Slip the group of warp pairs off the peg. Holding the front of the warp under consistent tension, wind the warp onto the back beam. Use paper, corrugated cardboard, or flat sticks to separate the layers, which will maintain even tension and prevent the layers from sticking together. Continue winding, inserting paper or sticks as necessary and holding the warp under tension, until the loops reach the front beam.

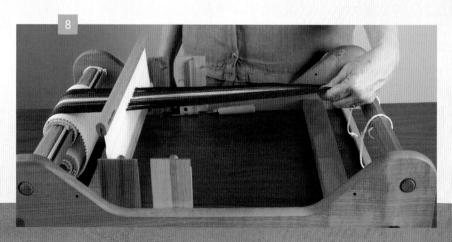

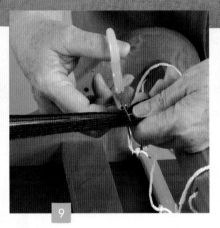

9 Cut the loops in the front of the warp.

10 Begin threading the holes. Insert the threading hook through the hole to the right of the first threaded slot.

11 Pull one of the first pair of warps out of the slot and use the threading hook to pull it through the hole.

12 Repeat across the warps until all warp pairs are threaded with a slot, then a hole.

13 Tie the warps in bundles to the front beam. (It's best to do this in bundles of about 1" [2.5 cm] evenly distributed across the warp. Start with a bundle in the center and work alternately out to the sides.) Bring the bundle of warps over the beam, around, and under, and tie the tails on the top in the first half of a square knot. Repeat until all the warp bundles are tied. Pat across the warp threads to check them for even tension, adjust the ties on the bundles if necessary, and tie the second half of the knot.

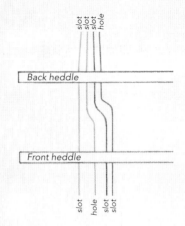

slot slot slot hole

Back heddle

Front heddle

slot hole slot slot

double heddle

Two heddles can be used to create a closer sett than would otherwise be possible with a single rigid heddle. Simply doubling the sett in a single heddle would create a different fabric structure (a half-basketweave) than the method below, which creates a plain weave.

When warping for the band on two heddles, you need to think about color order. Using this method, the two threads on the left in the front heddle will be the color on the left (see diagram at left). The thread through the hole in the back slot will be one of the right pair of threads in the weave structure. (You may find it helpful to alternate between two different colors for a striped pattern, using one loop of each in every slot, to see how the threads fall.)

1 Follow Steps 1–3 of Single Heddle. Take the second warp loop around the warp bar and thread it through the same slot as the first warp yarn and around the peg. Each slot will have 2 warp loops, or 4 warp threads. Continue until all warp loops are threaded in pairs. Follow Steps 5–9 of Single Heddle.

2 Begin threading the back heddle. With the threading hook, draw 1 thread from each slot through the hole to the right of the slot.

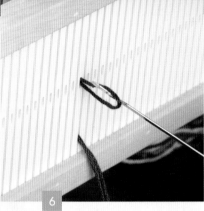

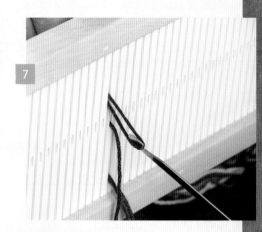

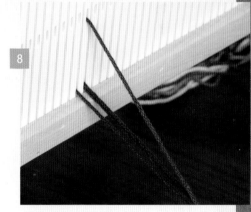

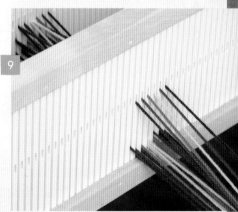

3 Continue across the heddle until all warps are threaded with 3 through each slot and 1 through the corresponding hole.

4 Mark the slot in the front heddle that aligns with the leftmost bundle of warp threads. This will be your leftmost threads pair in the final warping.

5 Add the second heddle in front of the first. Thread a pair of warps—1 from the hole and 1 of the slot warps—through the slot to the right of the leftmost slot.

6 Pick up the remaining pair from the back slot and thread 1 through the hole in the front heddle to the left of the slotted pair.

7 Thread the remaining warp in the slot to the left of the hole thread.

8 The 4 threads will be grouped as shown.

9 Thread a pair of warps (from the slot and hole of the back heddle) in the next slot to the right. Repeat Steps 6–7. Work across the warps until all threads are placed.

10 In each heddle, there will be 3 threads in each slot and 1 thread through each hole. Follow Step 14 of Single Heddle to tie warps in bundles onto the front beam.

11 Clear the sheds to make sure all the threads are in the right place, especially at first. Move heddles one by one to help clear the shed once. After you can see that the sheds are in place, the heddles move together as if they are one—both in the up shed or both in the down shed. (It may be helpful to lash the two heddles together at each end.)

warping for cardweaving on
four pegs

Weavers who are accustomed to floor looms with multiple heddles are probably more accustomed to measuring a warp on a warping board, then tying the warp onto the loom and threading the heddles. This technique is used for cardwoven bands throughout this book.

This method requires a little more equipment than the single-peg method; if a warping board isn't available, a set of four warping pegs or C-clamps will also work. Warping pegs are normally sold in a set with one single peg and a block with two pegs. Added to the warping peg that comes with your rigid-heddle loom, you have four pegs ready to set up. (Warping pegs are used here instead of a warping board because you may not have a warping board, but you may choose to use one instead.)

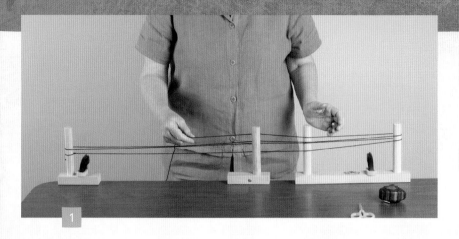

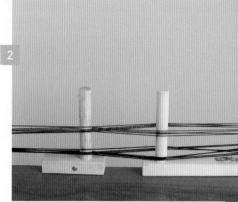

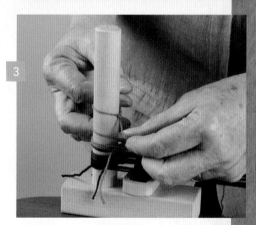

1. Set up the pegs to wind the necessary warp length. Tie the end of the first warp thread to the first peg and bring the thread to the last peg and back.

2. Make the cross as necessary. (For plain weave, you may alternate the cross on each length; for cardweaving, you may alternate after every two passes or 4 warp threads, as shown here.) We are warping in groups of 4 to facilitate threading cards for cardweaving, but we could also use pegs to warp the rigid heddle (either singly or in groups of two through the cross for one heddle or in groups of four for two heddles).

3. Change colors by tying the new color to the warping peg.

cross

The cross is a method for keeping threads wound on a warping board in the order in which they were wound. The cross is made by alternating in which direction the warp passes between two pegs.

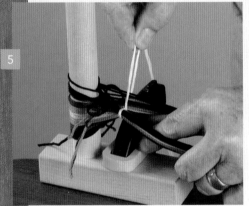

4 When the warp is wound, tie it securely through the cross.

5 Tie the ends of the warp with a figure eight.

6 Clamp the loom securely on table or in stand. Secure the warp bundle to the front of the loom or a peg.

7 Cut the other end of the warp.

8 Cut the tie securing the cross.

9. Thread the cards or heddle according to the draft or pattern. As you thread the cards, slide the 4-thread bundles out of the cross in order.

10. When the threading is complete, tie the warp onto the back apron bar or peg. If using a rigid-heddle loom, wind the warp from the front apron bar to the back, moving the cards or heddle as needed. When the end of the warp threads reach the front beam, cut the tie and ends. Adjust the tension as needed and tie the warp to the front beam. If using pegs, attach the warp to the pegs using a lark's head knot (10a and 10b).

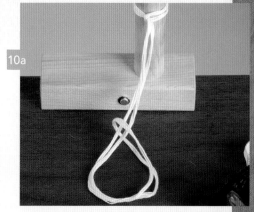

weaving on multishaft loom

Although the directions for these projects are written for a rigid-heddle loom, weavers with more complex looms can make any of the projects with a few adjustments:

1. Multishaft looms need a lot more yarn for loom and warping waste. Most of these projects suggest 18" (45.5 cm); multishaft weavers will calculate according to the looms they are using.

2. Instead of using two heddles for a closer sett, multishaft weavers can thread plain weave or straight draw on any number of shafts and use the reed that most easily accomodates the desired sett.

3. The multishaft weaver will still need to use a hand beater instead of or in addition to the loom's beater to ensure the firm beat these fabrics require.

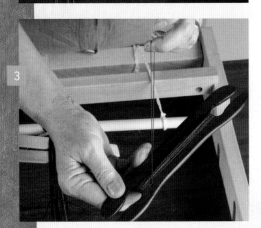

Shuttles are used to carry the weft yarn back and forth through the open shed of the warp yarns. Wind your shuttle carefully so that it unwinds without tangles and try not to crowd too much yarn on the shuttle. When the weft on your shuttle runs out, wind your shuttle with more yarn and lay the new yarn in the same space as the yarn which has run out. Overlap the two ends in the open shed, close the shed, beat, and continue weaving. You do not want a gap or space where there is no weft—it is the weft that holds the fabric together. This is true for every project in this book, even when the weft is not visible.

1   A netting shuttle is very convenient for hand-manipulated weaves. Begin winding a flat netting shuttle by wrapping the weft yarn around the inner "spike." Bring the weft yarn to the bottom and through the groove. Turn the shuttle over and bring the weft yarn up, around the inner "spike," and down back through the groove. Repeat until the shuttle is full or you have plenty of weft to work with.

2   A belt shuttle features a small hole that prevents the yarn from unwinding if you drop the shuttle. After winding the weft on the shuttle, pass the end through the hole.

3   To release weft yarn from the shuttle, pull a loop off the end of the shuttle and draw the slack through the hole.

plain
weave

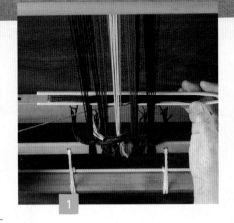

Plain weave is the simplest of weave structures and the most durable of fabrics. All threads alternate over and under in succession. There are no floating threads in either the warp or weft.

header

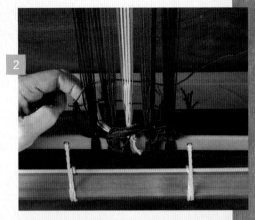

Pat across the warp with a flat hand to feel that the tension is even across the warp and adjust the knots if necessary. Weaving begins with a header, used to spread the warps into the proper weaving position after tying them to the front apron bar.

1. Open the shed by raising the heddle. Insert a length of weft, but do not beat with the heddle.

2. Change the shed and insert another length of weft, but again do not beat with the heddle. Change the shed again (raise the heddle for an open shed) and pass the weft a third time.

3. Beat the 3 wefts with the heddle.

4. The 3 weft passes will have begun to spread the warps. Check that the tension is even across the warp. Repeat 3 weft passes and beat until the warps are spread evenly.

using sticks in the warp

1 For fabric that will be beaten firmly with a hand beater (most of the projects in this book), open a shed and insert a stick or some rags.

2 Repeat Step 1 two more times to create a firm surface to beat against. Change the shed and begin weaving.

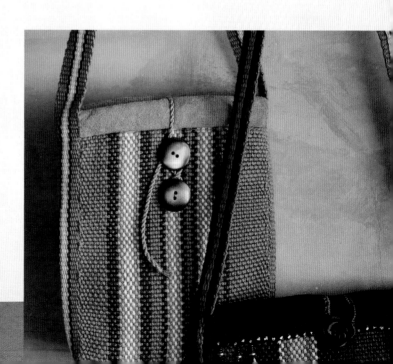

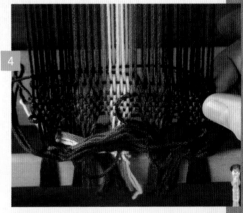

plain weave

1. After the header, begin weaving the hem of the textile by passing the weft in an open shed.

2. Pull the shuttle through, leaving a tail. Beat the weft in place with the heddle and change the shed. The method of beating varies with the type of fabric being woven, from pressing, as in the case of this fabric, to actually beating, as will be the case in some of the later techniques.

3. Tuck the tail end into the second shed.

4. Pass the shuttle through in the opposite direction with the second weft pass.

5. One technique to allow for extra weft so the fabric does not pull in at the selvedges is to insert the weft at an angle.

6 Alternately, "bubble" the weft to prevent the selvedge from pulling in.

7 Adjust the amount of weft in the shed so that the yarn does not bubble at the selvedges.

8 Continue to change the shed, pass the weft, and beat, repeating until you have woven the desired length of fabric for your project. Advance the warp (unroll from the back and roll on to the front) as needed. Because the warp threads in the holes may stretch out, it may be necessary to loosen and retighten the warp to adjust the tension.

how far can you weave?

I find it comfortable to weave to within 12" (30.5 cm) of the end of the warp. I can weave more if necessary, but it starts to become a struggle. Make sure each shed is clear, especially toward the end of the warp, before you pass the shuttle.

making cloth
into bags

Once the fabric is removed from the loom, it must be secured, washed, and prepared for constructing and finishing the bag.

wash

Secure the ends of each woven piece, either with a row of twining (see page 58) before taking it off the loom or by machine sewing it using the zigzag attachment.

Wash each woven piece when it comes off the loom, either by hand or machine. To wash by hand, fill a tub with hot water and a splash of detergent, then submerge the textile and let it soak for a while. Empty the soapy water and fill another tub with clear hot water to rinse. Check regularly to make sure no color is running from the yarns. If there is any color in the water, take out the bag and rinse it. If color is running, use a dye magnet to capture the excess dye. I also use Synthrapol when washing yarns I haven't tested.

Rinse until the water is clear of suds, then spin out the excess water in the spin cycle of a washer or press out the water with a towel. Lay the fabric flat to dry or press the slightly damp fabric and bands with a warm iron. For the plain-weave bags, iron interfacing to the back of the fabric to stiffen it. Choose a weight based on your intended use and how firm you want the bag to be. (Knotted pile is treated a bit differently; see page 105.)

construction

Finishing techniques will vary depending on the bag you are making. You may have other ideas that are just as appropriate. These basic directions are used to assemble the bags except as otherwise directed.

Different weights and varieties of interfacing are available for a range of fabrics.

finish edges

The raw edges of the fabric need to be covered or secured. I like to use leather and velvet trims for my bags.

Cut a piece of leather, velvet, or other fabric at least 1" (2.5 cm) longer than the width of the fabric. Cut a piece of thin batting to fit the edge of the fabric. Lay the fabric right side up with the leather wrong side up, centered across the width of the fabric, with the top edges aligned. Center the batting over the width of the fabric aligned with the finished edge. Sew through all three layers parallel to the top edge, leaving about ¼" (6 mm) seam allowance (as shown above and at left).

Fold the leather up so that the right sides of the leather and fabric are facing. Fold the excess leather around the sides of the fabric. Fold the leather and batting to the back of the fabric over the top edge so that the wrong sides are together. With the right side of the fabric facing, sew just below the folded leather. Whip-stitch along the edges of the leather. Repeat for the other end.

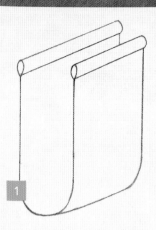

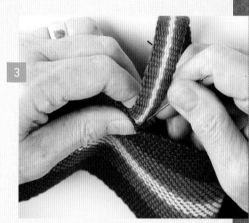

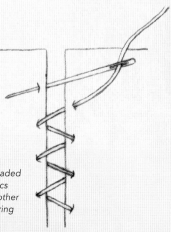

attach band

The bands for several of the projects in this book are sewn to the edges of the bag fabric.

1 Fold the bag body in half with the finished edges together and right sides facing out. Mark the center (bottom) of the folded fabric along each side.

2 Place one end of the band perpendicular to the fabric centered over the bottom (so that the underside of the fabric with interfacing shows).

3 Use a baseball stitch to sew the band to the bottom of the bag.

4 Fold the fabric and band to meet edge to edge. Stitch the band to the fabric from bottom to top along both sides of the band. Repeat along the other edge of the fabric, being careful not to twist the band.

To work baseball stitch, bring the threaded needle down through one of the fabrics to be joined, then down through the other piece to be joined. The stitches will bring the edges together.

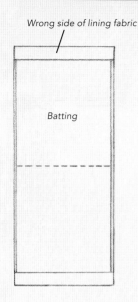

Wrong side of lining fabric

1

Batting

2

3

lining

Choose a lining material that complements the woven fabric, either in color, pattern, or theme. Sometimes a contrast fabric is useful; light fabrics are used when I will need to see into the bag. Dark fabrics are fine for small bags that will hold a cell phone or one small item. If the bag fabric is floppy or thin, a layer of thin batting gives the bag enough body to hold up under use. Some of the bag fabrics are firm and thick enough to give the bag itself some body.

1 Cut a piece of lining fabric at least 3" (7.5 cm) longer and 1" (2.5 cm) wider than the finished size of the lining. Cut a layer of batting 1" (2.5 cm) less than the length of the bag. Lay the lining wrong side up and center the batting on it, then sew the lining and batting together at the midpoint to prevent slipping.

2 Fold the lining and batting with the right sides of the fabric facing in. Sew up the sides. Trim the fabric close to the seams, leaving about ¼" (6 mm) seam allowance.

3 Gussets: Fold the bottom corners of the lining out to square the bottom of the lining. The amount of fabric folded out depends on the width of the bag. For a lining that fits snugly inside but not too tight, make the fold about ¼" (6 mm) shorter than the inside width of the bag at the bottom corners (taking the batting into account). Stitch across the corners and trim off the excess fabric, leaving about ¼" (6 mm) seam allowance.

4 Fold the excess lining fabric over the top edge of the envelope and insert the lining into the bag. Handstitch the lining to the top of the bag.

button closure

If your bag is to have a button and button loop, use one of the weaving yarns or other coordinating yarn to make a buttonhole loop attached to the back of the bag. Mark the location of the loop. With strong thread and an appropriate needle, pass through the fabric to make a loop big enough to accommodate the button, leaving a tail; repeat the thread path twice more to make a strong foundation. Use the buttonhole stitch to sew over the loop around its circumference, covering the tail. Secure the ends of the thread. Sew a button to the front.

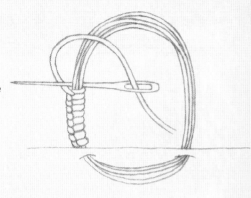

Buttonhole stitch

twisted cord

To make a strong and decorative cord for closure, cut a length of yarn more than twice as long as your desired finished cord. Secure one end of the yarn and twist the other end until the yarn begins to kink up. Holding the end firm so that the twist does not escape, fold the yarn in half and allow the ends to wrap around each other. Tie the ends together with an overhand knot to capture the twist.

Twisted cord

first bags

this first project is a series of bags in plain-weave fabric with warp-faced plain-weave bands. It is a good project to help you become accustomed to the equipment if you are new to weaving on a rigid heddle or have not used these yarns before. Plain weave is an honest, simple cloth; the threads follow the classic over-under-over-under construction that most people think of as woven cloth. Color becomes an important feature of the fabric, as do fiber choice, yarn size, sett, and finishing methods.

The yarn is the same throughout the fabric: durable, practical cotton, easy to wash if necessary. The fabric is woven with one heddle, and the bands, which are a closer sett, are woven with two heddles.

project information

yarns:
Fabric—Tahki Cotton Classic (warp and weft). Band—Tahki Cotton Classic (warp); 10 crochet cotton, 5/2 cotton, or DMC cotton (weft).

heddles:
Fabric—one 12- or 12.5-dent. Band—two 10-dent.

sett:
Fabric—12–12.5 epi. Band—20 epi.

finished measurements:
Fabric—3¾" x 10" (9.5 x 25.5 cm). Band—1" x 45" (2.5 x 114.5 cm).

other materials:
One shuttle; iron-on interfacing; measuring tape; sewing machine; matching sewing thread; handsewing needle; tapestry needle; lining fabric; leather, suede, velvet, or other fabric trim; quilt batting (optional); button for closure; beads or embellishments (optional).

bag
fabric

I chose to use a heavy weft, the same yarn as the warp, for these bags. A heavier weft will make a heavier fabric, and fine weft will make a more supple fabric.

warping plan

Following the instructions for warping with a single heddle (see page 21), set up the loom so that the warp beam is at least 40" (101.5 cm) from peg. Beginning 13 slots over from the center of the heddle, sley (or thread) 27 pairs of warp threads in slots as follows: 7 slots/rust, 4 slots/orange, 1 slot/bright orange, 3 slots/yellow, 1 slot/bright orange, 4 slots/orange, 7 slots/rust. Wind the warp onto the back beam using sticks, paper, or corrugated paper for warp packing. Cut the pairs in front of the heddle and thread the holes with one of the pair of warps from each slot. Secure the warp to the loom. Weave a header and wind the Tahki Cotton Classic weft yarn on a shuttle.

weaving

Use the rigid heddle to place the weft with the shed still open. This allows control of the yarn at the selvedge and easy removal and reinsertion of the weft if the selvedge is too loose or too tight. A second beat on a closed shed is also recommended.

Weave until the fabric measures 10" (25.5 cm) or desired length. Check your work as you progress. Mistakes made with this smooth, firm yarn are easy to see while weaving. If the weft skips over or under a warp thread (or several!), it is easy to unweave. The cotton yarn holds up well to unweaving and re-weaving, even for several inches. Cut the fabric from the loom, wash, and iron it.

warping math

Fabric width: 3¾" (9.5 cm) x 12 epi = 45 ends
• Add 20% for draw-in and shrinkage = 54 ends = 27 pairs of warps.

Fabric length: 10" (25.5 cm)
• Add 20% (2" [5 cm]) for take-up and shrinkage = 12" (30.5 cm)
• Add 18" (45.5 cm) for loom waste and warping waste = 30" (76 cm)
• Add 10"–30" (25.5–76 cm) for sampling = 40"–60" (101.5–152.5 cm)

Final calculations:
54 ends and 40"–60" (101.5–152.5 cm) warp for finished fabric 3¾" (9.5 cm) wide and 10" (25.5 cm) long.

band

Weft size matters in both the fabric and the band. The warp yarn for the band is the same as for the fabric. In general, in a warp-faced fabric, the more shots per inch, the firmer the band will feel. The color only shows at the selvedge where you turn the weft.

warping plan

Following the directions for single-peg double-heddle warping (see page 24), set up the loom so that the back beam is at least 75" (190.5 cm) from the peg. Beginning 8 slots over from the center of the first heddle, thread

2 warp loops per slot in 16 slots. Wind the warp, using paper, sticks, or corrugated cardboard for packing. Thread both heddles and secure the warp to the loom. Wind a shuttle with the weft yarn and weave a header.

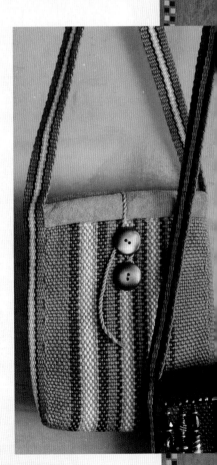

warping math

Band width = 1" (2.5 cm) x 20 epi = 20 ends.
Add 50% to make the fabric warp-faced = 30 ends; subtract 2 ends (to balance the number of threads on each heddle) = 28 ends.

- Finished length: 45" (114.5 cm)
- Add 20% (9" [23 cm]) for take-up = 54" (137 cm)
- Add 5% (about 3" [7.5 cm]) for shrinkage = 57" (145 cm)
- Add 18" (45.5 cm) for loom and warping waste = 75" (190.5 cm) on the loom

Final calculations: 28 ends x 75" (190.5 cm) for a finished band 1" (2.5 cm) wide and 45" (114.5 cm) long.

weaving

Lock in the tail end of the weft thread on the first shot (see Fig. 1). Bands are close-sett for durability. This warp-faced fabric is 28 ends, pulled in to a band of less than 1". (You can use an inkle loom if you have one.) You will have to pull in on the weft to make the band warp-faced, which takes a little practice (see Fig. 2).

Lift both heddles together to make one shed and drop both heddles together to make the other shed. In a warp-faced weave structure like these bands, the warp undulates over and under the weft, creating a greater amount of take-up in the warp as you weave. Weave with loose enough tension so that the warps can rise and fall over and under the wefts as they are inserted and so that you will be able to pull in the warps to maintain the same width in the band as you weave. You will have to advance the warp more often than for the plain weave fabric of the body of the bag. When weaving bands, tension should be tight enough to help clear the shed, but not so tight as to deflect the weave structure (the over and under of the warp face).

As you weave, make sure to pull the weft close to the selvedge at each pass. Check your band for consistent width as you work (see Fig. 3). When you have woven the desired length, weave in the end of the weft yarn with a needle, in the same path as the previous two weft passes (see Fig. 4).

construction

When the fabric is cut off the loom, use the zigzag stitch on the sewing machine to secure the edges of both ends. Wash and dry the fabric in a regular cycle in the washing machine and dryer. I pull the fabric out slightly damp and press with a warm iron to finish the drying and remove any wrinkles. Iron the interfacing to the wrong side of the fabric according to the manufacturer's directions.

Soak or wash the band, then press it dry with a warm iron. Follow the directions on page 35 to finish the edges of the fabric and assemble the bag.

first bag series

Since the loom and yarns were new to me and I wanted to practice using them, I made seven bags. After the first two, I became accustomed to the equipment and yarns and made the rest as color samples, watching how the colors interacted in the woven fabrics. I find it useful, when learning anything new, to make a series of projects that vary slightly, giving a better overview of the process, the materials, of problems and possible solutions.

The bags all use the same yarns and same sett in different colorways. They can be used as small bags by themselves, as a container for all kinds of small things: MP3 players, cell phones, travel documents, or as an organizer in a larger bag. I varied the size of the bags by changing the width and length of the woven fabric and the bands: narrow or wide fabrics, short or long bands, and one band has a clip to attach it to a belt loop or purse handle.

The number of warp ends determines how wide your finished bag will be. The sample bag measures 3¾" (9 cm) wide when finished; for a wider bag, increase the number of warp ends—at 12 ends per inch, a 10" (25.5 cm) wide bag would have 120 ends.

Band length also varies depending on the end use of your bag. Most of the bags here have a band length of between 45 and 60 inches. You can always cut a band shorter if you decide your bag needs a short handle, but they do not stretch, so be sure to weave enough.

pick-up
weaving

·········

woven bands can be decorative as well as functional.

Pick-up bands are among my favorite bands to weave; pick-up patterning is easier to do than it looks, and the process can be adapted to the rigid-heddle loom. The Pick-up Tote and Spiral Star Bag both use pick-up bands for their handles. This is one of my favorite weave structures—it is simple to weave, requires nothing other than fingers (or sticks, but I use fingers), and looks fabulously difficult.

materials

yarns:
Warp—Tahki Cotton Classic, white and black. Weft—Tahki Cotton Classic, white.

heddle:
One 8-dent.

tools:
One shuttle; tapestry needle.

yarns

Two warp yarns are needed for this patterning: background and pattern warps. The pattern warps in this form of pick-up band are usually twice the size of the background warps. You can either use two different yarns for the two sizes you will need or double the warps in the pattern area; in this sampler the warps are doubled.

This sample band uses Tahki Cotton Classic in high-contrast colors—black and white—so that we can easily track where all the yarns are going. If the weft color is the same as the warp, as in this sampler, it will not add another element. With a contrasting color, the weft spots can make a supplementary design among the pick-up patterns.

Weft size matters in weaving these bands. Properly woven, they will be tight and the pattern will be distinct; using a fine weft is generally the best way to accomplish this. The bands for the projects are woven tighter with a smaller weft, but this sampler uses a large weft yarn—the same Cotton Classic as the warp, in white—so that each row of weaving will be distinct.

To accommodate the doubled warp threads, set up a loom with an 8-dent heddle.

The graph below is how a pick-up threading draft is traditionally noted:

| W | | W | | W | | W | | | W | | W | | | W | | W | | | W | | | W | W | | W | | W | | 1 |
| W | | W | | W | | | | W | | W | | | W | | W | | | W | | W | | | W | | | W | | W | | W | | 2 |

- W   Background (1 white thread)
- ■   Pattern (2 black threads)
- □   Pattern area

This draft indicates a two-shaft weave structure—each horizontal row of symbols represents one shaft in the setup. In a rigid-heddle loom, those two shafts are the holes (1) and the slots (2) in one heddle.

The solid squares are the pattern yarn (black), and the other squares are the plain weave warps (white). This draft indicates a 6-thread plain-weave border, then an area with 7 pattern units (each containing 2 black threads) with plain weave in between, followed by a 6-thread plain-weave border, for a total of 38 warp ends. In several places there are 2 threads in a hole or slot in the heddle; the spaces in an

8-dent heddle are large enough to accommodate both threads.

Patterns like these are geometrically progressive—each warp pick-up follows the previous in geometric succession. Soon you will be able to weave them without looking at the graph.

warp for
the band

1 Following the instructions for single-peg single-heddle warping (see page 21), start threading on the left 10 slots over from the center of the heddle with the plain-weave border in holes and slots for the first 6 threads, then thread 2 pattern warps in one slot, followed by one plain weave warp in a hole, one plain weave warp in a slot, then 2 pattern warps in a hole. Continue across, following the draft.

2 Insert sticks at the beginning of the weaving and weave a small header (see directions on page 31).

3 The band is threaded at 3½" (9 cm) wide through the heddle. The rigid heddle holds the warps spaced wider than you want your finished band, so you will need to pull that width in as you weave. Weave for a while to practice maintaining a uniform width of about 1⅜" (3.5 cm) as you work.

- ⊡ Pattern (black) dropped down
- ■ Pattern (black) on surface
- ☐ Background (white) thread on surface

plain
weave

After you have established the width of the band, begin the pick-up following the pattern diagram. Read the chart row by row, starting at the bottom. The black squares indicate that a black pair of warps should be on the top; white squares are where the plain weave warps and the weft are showing on the surface.

If no threads are picked up or dropped (for Rows 1–7), the weave structure will look speckled. The pattern is not truly plain weave because the pattern threads are doubled. The weft shows on the surface where it goes over the doubled threads, creating another design element if you choose.

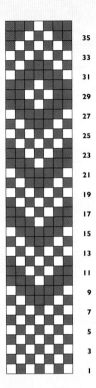

35
33
31
29
27
25
23
21
19
17
15
13
11
9
7
5
3
1

picking up
warp threads

1 After several rows of weaving, the pattern diagram shows a dark "V" design, beginning with Row 8. As you drop the heddle, several of the marked pattern pairs come up automatically.

2 To make the design, some pattern threads must be picked up. Pick up only the center pair, making the band look like this. Pass the weft, change the shed, and beat the weft into place.

3 To pick up pattern pairs, hold the warps of the up shed in your hand, spread them where you need to pick up a pair, reach down, and pull the warps to the top layer.

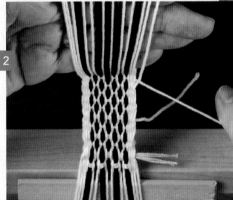

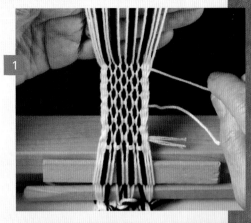

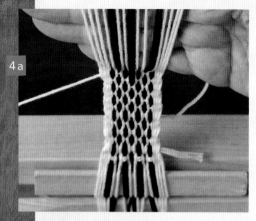

4a

4b

5

4   With the heddle up, the opposite pattern pairs come up automatically (4a). You can see that center pair, which you picked up in Step 3, is still up. The pattern indicates that 5 pairs should be up, so you'll need to pick up 2 more pairs (4b). Pass the weft, change the shed, and beat the weft into place.

5   On the next row, the pattern calls for 3 pairs on either side of the center to be up. Pick up the indicated pairs, pass the weft, change the shed, and beat.

6   Continue to follow the pattern, picking up pattern pairs where necessary. The surface design on the band should look like the pattern graph.

dropping
warp threads

At the top of the pattern draft, beginning with Row 38, there is a circle symbol indicating that pattern threads must be dropped down. This will create a band without the speckled background characteristic of this weave structure.

⊡   Pattern (black) dropped down
■   Pattern (black) on surface
□   Background (white) thread on surface

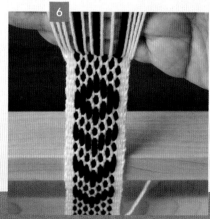

6

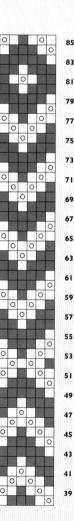

85
83
81
79
77
75
73
71
69
67
65
63
61
59
57
55
53
51
49
47
45
43
41
39

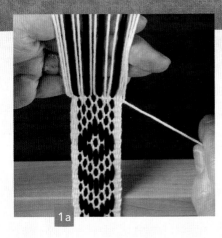

The process of weaving this section is similar to the pick-up portion, except that in addition to pulling threads up from the layer below, we will also push threads down to the lower part of the shed and out of the way.

1. Row 38 has 4 pattern threads that come up in the shed (1a), but Row 38 of the pattern indicates 3 pairs right in the center. Drop the outside 2 pairs and pick up 1 pair in the center of the band (1b). Pass the weft, change sheds, and beat as usual.

2. In the next row (Step 6 on previous page), 3 pairs come up, and you will need to drop the 2 outside pairs.

3. The next few rows will have pick-ups, drops, or both, and the pattern will gradually develop without the speckled background. You may see the weft in the space created by the dropped pair.

If the chart shows no pick-ups or drops, simply pass the weft. Continue to follow the graph, either picking up the pattern threads onto the surface of the band or dropping them out of the way, creating the sampler.

When you have finished weaving, cut the band off the loom. Use a tapestry needle to weave in the weft end.

pick-up
tote

·······

tote bags are handy storage and carrying containers for knitting and sewing projects, a picnic and a book, or any must-have items for your day. To be useful, a tote bag needs to be large enough to hold what you need, be durable, and allow easy access to the contents. Plain-weave fabric is the most durable of weave structures: there are no floats to catch yarn, and a lot of close intersections of warp and weft bind the fabric together.

This fabric is plain-weave cotton, firmly woven and made as durable as possible by a firm beat. To accomplish this, use a separate handheld beater to firmly pack the weft in place. Place the weft with the heddle as usual, then push the weft more firmly in place with the beater.

project information

yarns:
Fabric and bands—Tahki Cotton Classic in three colors (warp); Aunt Lydia's Size 10 Classic Crochet Cotton (weft).

heddles:
Fabric—two 10-dent. Band—one 8-dent.

sett:
Fabric—20 epi. Band—8 epi.

finished measurements:
Fabric—14" (35.5 cm) wide and 30" (76 cm) long. Bands—each 1¼" (3.2 cm) wide and 36" (91.5 cm) long.

other materials:
One shuttle; handheld beater; measuring tape; lining fabric; firm iron-on interfacing (for bag); batting; lighter-weight interfacing (for pockets); matching sewing thread; sewing machine; sewing needle; tapestry needle.

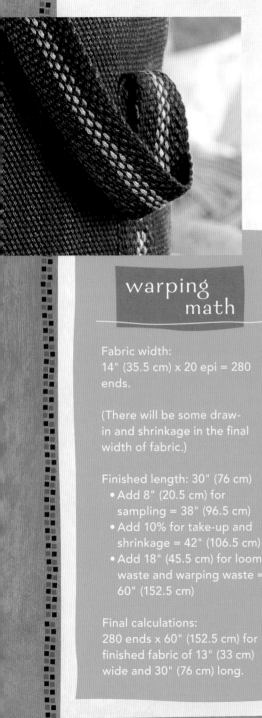

bag fabric

I would like a closer sett (24 ends per inch on two 12-dent heddles), but the yarn is too heavy to handle easily on this loom at that sett, so I sett the bag at 20 ends per inch. The fabric will be reinforced with iron-on interfacing to make it firmer and prevent knitting needles, crochet hooks, and other tools from poking through the bag.

warping plan

Set up the loom so that the warp beam is at least 60" (152.5 cm) from the peg. Warp the loom following the directions for warping two heddles (see page 24), beginning 35 slots over from the center point and threading loops through the heddle around the peg following this color pattern: 44 loops blue (B), 2 loops purple (P), 2B, 1P, 1B, 1 loop red (R), 1B, 2P, 2R, 1B, 2P, 1B, 3R, 2P,1R, 1P, 3R; reverse the threading direction. Wind the warp onto the back beam using sticks as packing material; they will provide a firmer resistance during beating and do not break down with heavy beating. Thread both heddles and secure the warp to the loom. Pay close atten-

tion that the warps threaded from the slot in the back heddle through the left slot and hole on the front heddle are the ones that you want on the left in your pattern. Wind a shuttle with the weft yarn and weave a header.

weaving

Weave a length of plain-weave fabric at the beginning as a sample and to establish the draw-in. Practice placing the weft with the heddle and using the separate hand beater. When you are satisfied with the consistency, weave about 34" (86.5 cm). Cut the fabric from the loom, wash, and iron it (see page 35).

warping math

Fabric width:
14" (35.5 cm) x 20 epi = 280 ends.

(There will be some draw-in and shrinkage in the final width of fabric.)

Finished length: 30" (76 cm)
• Add 8" (20.5 cm) for sampling = 38" (96.5 cm)
• Add 10% for take-up and shrinkage = 42" (106.5 cm)
• Add 18" (45.5 cm) for loom waste and warping waste = 60" (152.5 cm)

Final calculations:
280 ends x 60" (152.5 cm) for finished fabric of 13" (33 cm) wide and 30" (76 cm) long.

pick-up
band

Because the bands are woven on one warp and cut apart, there is extra warping waste allowed for the area that will be cut. There will also be some unwoven warp as fringe on the bands, requiring additional warp.

■ ■ ▨ ▨ Pattern (2 threads of color indicated)
■ Background (1 blue thread)
□ Pattern area

warping plan

Following the directions for warping a pick-up band (see page 48), set up the loom so that the back beam is at least 96" (244 cm) from the peg. Follow the draft above for color placement and number of warps. Use a doubled warp for the pattern threads as for the pick-up sampler (see page 46), threading 6 blue threads at the border, then 9 pattern pairs alternating with 8 pairs of plain weave, then the remaining border threads, for 48 threads total.

Wind the warp, using paper, sticks, or corrugated cardboard for packing. Insert sticks at the beginning of the warp. Wind a shuttle with the weft yarn and weave a header.

warping math

Finished width: 1¼" (3.2 cm) = 46 ends (pulled in during weaving)

Finished length: 36" (91.5 cm) per band = 72" (183 cm)
 • Add 5% (4" [10 cm]) for take-up and shrinkage = 76" (193 cm)
 • Add 20" (51 cm) for loom and warping waste = 96" (244 cm)

Final calculations:
 52 ends x 96" (244 cm) for two finished bands, each 1¼"
 (3.2 cm) wide and 36" (91.5 cm) long.

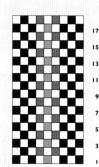

Inverted V (left)

Plain Weave (middle)

V (right)

Pattern chart numbers (left band, bottom to top): 1, 3, 5, 7, 9, 11, 13, 15, 17, 19, 21, 23, 25, 27, 29, 31, 33, 35, 37, 39, 41, 43, 45, 47, 49, 51, 53, 55, 57, 59, 61, 63, 65, 67, 69, 71, 73, 75

Middle chart numbers: 1, 3, 5, 7, 9, 11, 13, 15, 17

Right chart numbers (bottom to top): 1, 3, 5, 7, 9, 11, 13, 15, 17, 19, 21, 23, 25, 27, 29, 31, 33, 35, 37, 39, 41, 43, 45, 47, 49, 51, 53, 55, 57, 59, 61, 63, 65, 67, 69, 71, 73, 75

◉ Pattern thread dropped down

■ ■ ■ ■ ■ Pattern thread on surface

☐ Background thread on surface

weaving

Lock in the end of the weft thread on the first shot and weave a few inches to establish the width; this section will be cut off later. Following the pattern at left, weave the V pattern (about 8" [20.5 cm]), then 20" (51 cm) of plain weave. (To find the length accurately, pin the tape measure to band.) End with 8" (20.5 cm) of the inverted V pattern. With a tapestry or sewing needle, pass the weft end along the weft thread of the last several rows of weaving to lock in the weft thread. Weave about 2" (5 cm) with some waste yarn to leave space between the two bands, then repeat the band pattern for the second band. Secure the weft thread with a needle.

When you have woven both bands, cut them from the loom and cut them apart. Wash the band, dry it, and press flat with a warm iron.

equal tension

The pick-up bands measure 37" (94 cm) under tension, but they measure 36" (91.5 cm) off the loom. The actual length of these two bands is not critical as long as they match. Choose which way to measure, then be consistent with both bands.

construction

Cut a piece of firm interfacing to fit the bag fabric and iron it in place (following the manufacturer's directions).

Lay the bag fabric flat with the right side facing up and pin the handles in place along both ends of the fabric (as illustrated below) so that the handles are just outside the central striped area of the bag fabric. Sew the handles in place with top stitches, reinforcing as needed with additional rows of stitching, to 3" (7.5 cm) from the ends of the fabric. (The top edges will be turned down and stitched once the sides are sewn in place.)

Iron the lining fabric and cut it to the measurements of the woven fabric. Attach pockets, if desired (see right). Cut a piece of batting to the same dimensions.

With the wrong sides of the lining fabric and woven fabric held together and the batting sandwiched between, sew the lining to the woven fabric around all the edges with zigzag or straight stitches. The lining and bag fabric will be handled as one piece from now on.

With the right side of the lining facing out, sew the side seams of the bag. Fold and sew triangle gussets (see page 38) to shape the bottom, making the bottom of the bag 4" (10 cm) wide. Fold over the top edge 1" (2.5 cm) twice and topstitch at least two rows around the top edge.

(see page 38)

pockets (optional)

If you would like pockets inside your bag, mark the position of two pockets on the lining fabric.

Iron lighter-weight interfacing to wrong side of lining fabric to correspond with pockets (following manufacturer's instructions) to reinforce the pocket seams.

Cut out fabric for pockets, leaving at least ¼" (6 mm) to fold under along both sides and the bottom.

Hem the top of the pockets.

Press ¼" (6 mm) under along the sides and bottom of the pockets and sew them to the right side of the lining fabric.

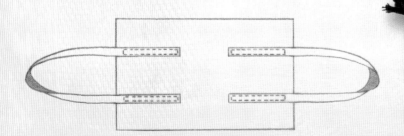

twining

....

I start and end many woven pieces with a row of twining. It helps set the spacing for the project, creates a firm edge at the beginning, and secures the wefts during the finishing process. I also use twining periodically in hand-manipulated fabric to re-establish the width—a row of twining can help prevent a fabric from pulling in or bowing out. Start with a sampler to learn single and double twining.

materials

yarn:
Crochet cotton (warp and weft); Tahki Cotton Classic (twining).

heddle:
One 8- or 10-dent.

tools:
One shuttle; hand beater.

yarns

The warp of this sampler will not show at all in the finished piece. The high twist of crochet cotton makes it strong and durable, even with the added abrasion of a hand beater. The Tahki Cotton Classic has a firm twist and high sheen for an attractive surface; choose two colors to see the twining.

warp

Set up the warp for the sampler as if to work plain weave. Using the single-peg single-heddle method (see page 21), set up a short warp of about 15" (38 cm). Use flat sticks as a warp packing material for this technique to keep the warp tension firm; paper and cardboard do not hold the tension as well as sticks. Thread the heddle and tie to the front beam. Weave a small header with crochet cotton to spread the warps (see page 31).

Repeat the three-shed header process as many times as needed until the warp is spread, then insert several flat sticks in alternating sheds to create a firm surface for beating.

single-color twining

Twining is worked on a closed shed, with the heddle in a neutral position.

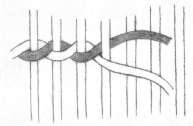

1. Cut 2 lengths of twining yarn, each about 6" (15 cm) longer than the width of the warp, and tie a knot to join two ends (or cut a single length 12" (30.5 cm) longer than the width of the warp). Place 1 length above the first warp; the second end will lie under the same warp. The end that is on top of the warps is the working end.

2. Pick up the working end and tuck it under the next warp. Bring the thread that was below the first warp to the top.

3. The other thread has now become the working end; it is taken over the top and wraps around the next warp end.

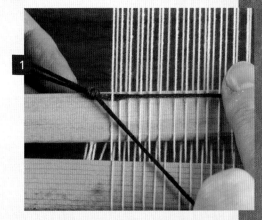

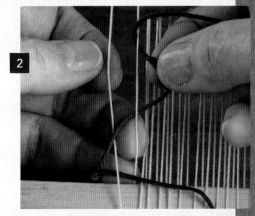

4 Continue across the warp, wrapping each end in turn around the successive warps, until all the warps have been wrapped. Keep the twining thread under tension and periodically adjust the tension so that all the wraps look even. Tie a knot close to the finishing edge.

5 Use the hand beater to push all the wraps close to the sticks.

6 Wind a small shuttle with crochet cotton for weft and work a few inches in plain weave before practicing double twining. Insert the first weft, leaving a tail; fold the tail into the next shed. Continue for a few inches of plain weave, beating the weft securely in place with the hand beater.

two-color twining

Two-color twining can be done the same way as single-color twining, twisting and wrapping each warp end with alternating colors and working back and forth. It can also be worked with two loops of yarn. More than one row of two-color twining can make patterns on the surface, depending on how the colors are used.

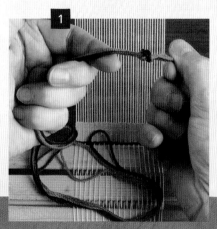

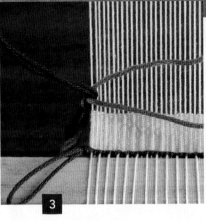

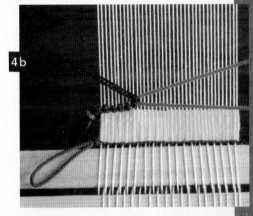

1 Cut 2 lengths of twining yarn, each about 12" (30.5 cm) longer than the width of the warp, and fold them in half. Holding the yarns together, tie an overhand knot near the end.

2 Place 1 pair at the edge of the warp over the first warp thread with the second pair under the first warp thread.

3 Bring the second pair up between the first 2 warps and insert through the loop of the top pair. Pass the next loop down between the warps and bring it up through the top loop.

4 Continue across, passing one loop under a warp (4a) then up and through the second loop (4b), which then goes around and under the next warp, until all the warps are covered.

5 Tie a knot close to the selvedge and beat with the hand beater. The edge is now not only decorative, it also secures the wefts and helps stabilize the sett.

twined
portfolio

·······

we all have piles of papers, files of papers, stacks of papers, and folders of papers. Everywhere we have papers that need to be organized, papers that need to be corralled, and papers that need to go with us somewhere neatly and in order. A paperless society is not here yet, so I made this bag to hold papers. This is a document portfolio, with a few handmade twists: the design is based on a paper envelope, and the size and color were chosen to fit inside and go with my laptop carrying case.

The fabric is accented by a few rows of decorative twining. There are rows of single and double twining using a color that closely matches the weft, creating a textural surface for the flap of the portfolio.

project information

yarns:
Size 10 crochet cotton (warp and weft); Tahki Cotton Classic in 2 colors, one that complements the weft and one that contrasts (twining).

heddles:
Two 10-dent.

sett:
20 epi.

other materials:
One shuttle; hand beater; iron-on interfacing; fabric or leather trim; small piece of leather or fabric (for button backing); two buttons; matching sewing thread; darning needle; sewing machine; sewing needle; measuring tape; glover's needle.

finished measurements:
11" (28 cm) wide and 30" (76 cm) long (measured before sewing).

portfolio
fabric

The weave structure for this envelope bag is weft-faced, meaning the warp does not show at all. This makes a firm fabric, a good thing where abrasion might be expected. The weight of the yarns determines the pliability of the fabric. The warp is spaced wider than one would choose for a balanced fabric, and the weft is beaten firmly to completely cover the warp.

The finished bag needs to be wide enough to hold papers, which are normally 8½" × 11" (21.5 × 28 cm), and you want some ease in the size of the bag to be able to slip a stack of papers in and out. 12" (30.5 cm) on the loom allows for these factors.

warping math

Fabric width:
11" (21.5 cm) x 20 epi = 220 ends.

- Add 10% (22 ends) for draw-in and shrinkage = 242 ends; subtract 2 ends (to balance the number of threads on each heddle) = 240 ends.

Finished length: 30" (76 cm)
- Add 8" (20.5 cm) for sampling = 38" (96.5 cm)
- Add 10% for take-up and shrinkage = 42" (106.5 cm)
- Add 18" (45.5 cm) for loom waste and warping waste = 60" (152.5 cm)

Final calculations:
242 ends x 60" (152.5 cm) for finished fabric 11" (21.5 cm) wide and 30" (76 cm) long.

warping plan

Set up the loom so that the back beam is at least 60" from the peg. Warp the loom following the directions for warping two heddles (see page 24). Wind the warp onto the back beam using sticks as packing material; they will provide a firmer resistance during beating and do not break down with heavy beating. Thread both heddles and secure the warp to the loom.

Wind a shuttle with the weft yarn and weave a header. Insert sticks after the header for a firm beating surface.

weaving

Start the project with one row of single twining (see page 58) to secure the ends before the body of the fabric begins. Begin weaving with the crochet cotton; if desired, use a contrasting color hem for ½" (1.3 cm). Use the heddle to place the wefts, then push the weft down firmly with the hand beater about every four rows. Weave until fabric measures 23" (58.5 cm), then begin twining on the flap.

Using both colors of twining yarn, alternate rows of single twining, double twining, and plain weave, placing the colors as desired, until the fabric measures 28" (71 cm) on the loom. (If you wove a contrasting hem at the other end, you may want to weave one here for ½" [1.3 cm]). Secure the end of the warp in an open shed. Twine over all warps to secure the end of the fabric.

Cut the fabric from the loom. Wash in a tub of warm water and detergent. (There is no need to agitate the fabric; you mostly want to soak it in hot water to shrink the yarns in place.) Rinse it in a tub of clear water or just under the tap and press out most of the water. With a steam iron, press the fabric dry.

construction

The portfolio doesn't have a handle; it is simply folded over and stitched to create its shape.

edging

Finish both ends of the fabric with fabric or leather trim (see page 36). The wrong side of the flap will show when the portfolio is opened, so turn the raw edge of the trim fabric under before topstitching.

closure

The portfolio is closed with two buttons attached near the bottom of the portfolio. With the right side of the woven fabric facing, mark the place-

ment of the buttons with pins. Cut a small square of iron-on interfacing and apply it (following the manufacturer's instructions) to the wrong side of the fabric to reinforce where the buttons will be sewn. Sew a small square of leather or other sturdy fabric to cover the interfacing. Sew the buttons through all layers.

Thread 32" (81.5 cm) of crochet cotton on a tapestry needle and pass through the fabric at the end of the flap. Make a twisted cord (see page 39) for closure.

assemble

With the wrong sides of the fabric together, fold up the bottom edge of the portfolio. Sew the side seams either by hand (using a baseball stitch) or by machine. To close the portfolio, wrap the twisted cord around the buttons in a figure eight.

soumak

········

soumak is a weft-wrapping technique

used widely on flat-weave textiles by nomadic weavers of Central Asia. Soumak can be an allover pattern in itself, used to accent warp-faced weaves, or as a flat-weave area in a pile-weave structure. Weave a sampler to practice the techniques.

The technique makes a sturdy raised surface and is longwearing and suitable for strong, hard-use fabrics. The weft is active, warp is passive, and the structure is entirely hand manipulated. It is versatile; there is a wide variety of textures and patterning possible. The fabric density is determined by sett, weft choices, warp choices, and number of warps encircled. It is not technically weaving, as there is no interlacement of the warp and weft.

yarns

Like twining, soumak covers the warp threads entirely. Tahki Cotton Classic has firm twist and a smooth, shiny surface. The crochet cotton warp is durable and will be hidden by the soumak wrapping.

materials

yarn:
Size 10 crochet cotton (warp and foundation weft); Tahki Cotton Classic (soumak).

heddles:
Two 7.5- or 8-dent.

sett:
15 or 16 epi.

tools:
At least four shuttles; hand beater.

warp and
weave header

We will use soumak as a supplemental weft; if all the soumak wraps were removed, there would still be a cohesive fabric structure created by the warp and the foundation weft. The plain weave will stabilize the fabric and secure the rows of wrapping.

Following the directions for single-peg double-heddle warping (see page 24), set up the loom so that the back beam is about 36" (91.5 cm) from the peg. Warp two 7.5-dent heddles with 56 ends (or 28 pairs, about 4" [10 cm]).

Weave a header to establish the width of the warp, then insert sticks for a firm beating surface (see page 32).

Wind one shuttle with crochet cotton for the foundation weft and another with Tahki Cotton Classic for the soumak. With the soumak weft yarn, work a row of single twining. Check the weft yarn to determine that it can fit easily between the warp threads at the sett spacing, without deflecting warps or being too thin.

With crochet cotton, weave a short hem, using the hand beater to press the weft firmly in place. The crochet cotton will become the foundation weft.

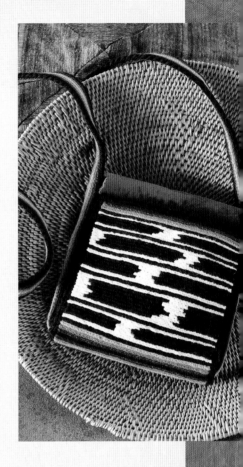

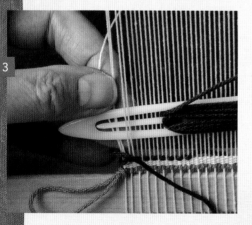

soumak

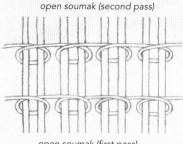

open soumak (second pass)

open soumak (first pass)

The look of soumak can be altered based on the number of ends wrapped, the direction of wrapping, the number of wraps of each group of warps, and whether there is a ground weft between rows. The soumak weft completely encircles the warp. As you weave, the warp may become stretched or feel less taut; adjust the tension as needed for consistency.

open soumak

The sampler starts at the bottom with the most common method of construction, known as open countered soumak. *Countered* means that the soumak is worked back and forth in alternating directions; if it were worked in the round, as for a basket, it would not be countered. We will work from the front of the weaving and wrap over 4 and back under 2 warps.

1 To begin the soumak weft, lay the intended weft yarn in an open shed for an inch or so, leaving a tail hanging in the back. Begin the soumak on the same edge where the foundation weft shuttle is so that both shuttles will be worked in the same direction. Close the shed.

2 Wrap the yarn around the first warp and the foundation weft thread (the crochet cotton, which is in place from the hem). Do not pull tightly; wraps should not deflect warps as you work. Use a light touch.

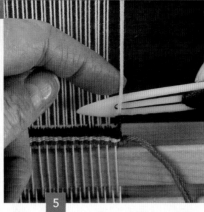

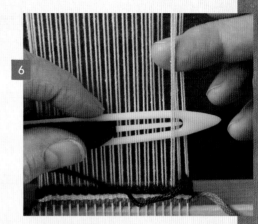

3   Working from left to right, wrap over 4 warp threads to the right, pass the shuttle to the back, and bring it up again 2 warp threads to the left, keeping the slack toward the front apron bar. (This might remind you of a backstitch.)

4   Repeat across to the right side of the warp, wrapping over 4 and under 2.

5   When you reach the right side of the weft, after passing up to the left of the last 2 warp threads, wrap that last (selvedge) pair once more. The selvedge will build up less than the center of the textile, so it is necessary to wrap the selvedges again at each turn. Try not to pull too tightly at this wrap. You may find that you need to wrap more than once to keep the selvedge even with the body of the work.

6   Turn and begin wrapping from right to left, passing down 4 threads from the right selvedge and up 2 threads over. Work all the way back to the left selvedge in the same over-4, under-2 pattern.

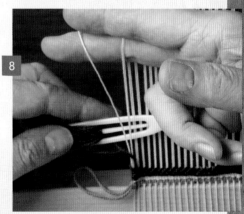

7   When you reach the left selvedge, wrap the final warp pair, including the foundation weft so it is covered and does not leave a loop at the edge.

8   Wrap the right selvedge pair and foundation weft again.

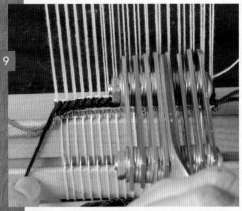

9 Raise the heddle and pass the foundation weft to the right; beat the weft in place, change the shed, and pass the foundation weft back to the left. (A soumak pass over and back followed by a foundation weft pass over and back constitutes one row of completed soumak.) Beat the soumak and foundation weft in place with the hand beater.

10 Begin a second row of soumak. Pass the foundation weft back and forth between each row.

When the soumak shuttle runs out of weft, lay the end in an open shed with a tail hanging in the back. Wind a new shuttle and begin the thread in the open shed, coming out at the point where the old weft left off, and continue. The two ends will be captured by the foundation weft and will nestle into the weave structure.

Weave for several more rows, then weave a small plain-weave section in crochet cotton before starting closed soumak.

adding and subtracting twist

The process of soumak adds or removes twist in the weft yarn, depending on which direction you are working and how the yarn is twisted. This can be seen in the finished appearance of the rows over long sections of soumak—one row looks tighter than the reverse direction; which direction this occurs in depends on the twist of the yarn. Over short distances, the twist decreases in one direction then increases on the reverse path, making the effect difficult to see. If the weft must travel over a wide area, you may wish to correct the twist issue by periodically dangling the shuttle to twist or untwist.

closed soumak

The second part of the sampler (gold) is closed-countered soumak. On the surface, it appears the same as the previous sample, but in closed soumak the weft passes *under* the wrap (closer to the front beam than the heddle).

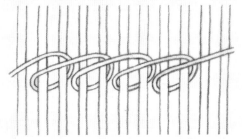

Row 1: left to right

If closed soumak is worked in both directions, the surface appears to be the same as the open soumak. The difference is that with each pass, the wrapping yarn is locked in place. This locked soumak is useful at the finishing edge of a textile.

1 Begin a new weft thread as for open soumak.

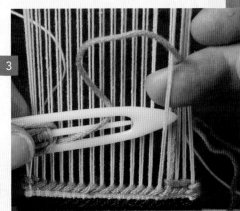

2 Wrapping the foundation weft as for open soumak, bring the soumak yarn over 4 warp threads to the right, bring the shuttle to the back, and bring the shuttle up 2 warp threads to the left of the foundation—but this time, bring the shuttle between the slack wrapping yarn and the weaving.

3 Work across from left to right in closed soumak. At the selvedge, wrap the selvedge pair at least once more and reverse the direction as in open soumak.

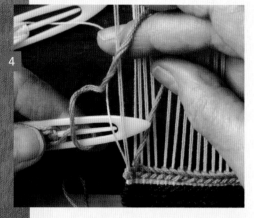

4 When you have woven back to the left edge, wrap the selvedge pair and foundation weft again.

5 Weave a short plain-weave section in crochet cotton before beginning the next section.

comparing open and closed soumak

Both open and closed soumak have the same surface appearance; in fact, they have the same structure. When worked in the same direction, the wraps slant in opposite directions, making it easy to change the surface appearance by switching back and forth between open and closed soumak (see Step 5, page 73). When changing back and forth, the yarn will twist or untwist continuously, so you will need to be aware and compensate by hanging the shuttle free to let the twist run in or out.

While techniques look the same when finished, there are a few differences in how they are worked and how they will behave when finished. Open soumak is easy to work on an upright loom with a full shuttle of yarn. It is locked in place with the plain-weave foundation weft. Closed soumak is harder to work on an upright loom because the weaver needs need to hold the working thread up and out of the way; it's easier on a horizontal loom. For a similar reason, it's harder to use a full shuttle of yarn with closed soumak, as the shuttle must fit between the warp and the loop of yarn held out of the way. It's easier to keep even tension in closed soumak, which locks the wraps in place as you work.

combined open and
closed soumak

If open soumak is worked in one direction and closed soumak is worked in the other, the fabric appears as if the soumak was always done in one direction instead of back and forth with different methods.

1 Begin a new weft thread and wrap the foundation weft.

2 Weave from left to right in open soumak: pass over 4 and under 2, keeping the slack yarn *below* the wraps.

3 At the right edge, wrap the selvedge pair once more.

4 Work from right to left in closed soumak: pass over 4 and under 2, keeping the slack yarn *above* the wraps.

5 Weave for several more rows so that the pattern becomes clear, passing the foundation weft between rows. Weave a short plain-weave section in crochet cotton before beginning the next section.

separate
selvedges

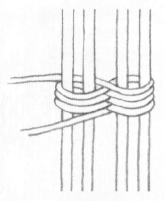

Even when wrapped with extra weft, selvedges done in soumak are not easy to keep even or neat. They are also not as structurally sound as the closely wrapped center section. In a rug or hard-use textile, this can be an issue; the selvedges can wear out or break down, causing the textile to fail. A solution to this is to use a rug technique: weave a separate selvedge yarn on each side in a figure eight.

1 Wind three shuttles of Tahki Cotton Classic (one for the soumak and one each for the selvedges). Lay all three tails in an open shed.

2 Bring the main shuttle up between the second and third pairs of warp threads and wrap the third pair before working across in open soumak.

Using a different color to wrap selvedges creates a tidy-looking border.

3 Continue across from left to right in open soumak, stopping before the last 2 warp pairs. Reverse direction and work back to the left, stopping with the first pair wrapped.

4 Use each selvedge shuttle to wrap a figure eight around the 2 warp pairs of the respective selvedges until the selvedges are level with the center portion. Be sure to include the foundation weft in the wrap on the left side.

5 Pass the foundation weft in both directions and beat in place. Weave a short plain-weave section before beginning the next section.

changing patterns

Soumak is usually wrapped over a regular number of warps; we have been using over four, under two. If this number varies, there is a change in the surface of the fabric, creating raised areas. Experiment with different combinations of warps to create surface texture in the soumak areas.

changing colors

Designs can be made in soumak by using more than one shuttle, each carrying a different color. Try a sampler of discontinuous colors.

1 Wind another shuttle for the additional color. Work open or closed soumak for several rows. When you reach the point where you want to change colors, lay the end of the new color in an open shed.

2 Begin soumak with the new yarn in the same direction as the previous color.

3 Wrap to the last 2 warp pairs, wrap the selvedges, and work back to the point where the new color was introduced.

4 Pick up the first color again and continue wrapping to the first edge.

5 Wrap the selvedges and weave the foundation weft as before, leaving the shuttle for each color waiting in front to be picked up on the next row.

6 As the colors advance, you may wish to vary the points where the color changes in each row.

7 Finish off the sample by inserting all the soumak and selvedge wefts into an open shed and weaving a hem. Beat closely with the hand beater so that the hem packs down the rows tightly. Finish with a row of twining.

floats

If one yarn needs to skip more than one pair of warps when changing colors, carry the excess yarn behind the work or start a new shuttle. Rugs should not have any floats along the back, as abrasion from use and wear will compromise the integrity of the rug over time. For lined articles, such as bags or pillow covers, floats do not pose a structural problem. If a long float will compromise the textile, start a new shuttle rather than carry the yarn.

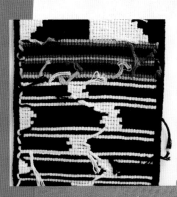

cardweaving

Cardweaving, or tablet weaving, is a twining technique in which groups of warps wrap around each other to form a twisted cord. A weft inserted at each twist holds several of these cords together in a narrow band, creating the characteristic surface texture of cardweaving. Cardweaving is actually a form of warp twining where the sheds are created by a pack of threaded cards. Warps are threaded through punched cards in groups of four, based on the color order of the band. Patterns in cardwoven bands depend on the color and the direction the warps travel through the holes in the cards and how the cards are turned.

materials

yarn:
Striped band—Tahki Cotton Classic (warp and weft); patterned band—crochet cotton (warp and weft).

heddle:
None.

tools:
Four warping pegs; fourteen four-hole cards; one shuttle.

yarns

The structure is warp-faced; the weft is insignificant and shows only slightly at the edges of the work. The yarns used for this technique need to be smooth, sturdy, and firmly twisted to be abrasion-resistant.

striped
band

This simple band has the same colors used in the Pinwheel Bag. Before weaving the entire length for the bag strap, practice working with the cards and maintaining even tension.

warp and header

Cardwoven bands are warped using the multiple-peg method (see page 26). For the first (striped) sample, we will use the warping pegs to hold the tension while weaving. Fourteen cards are threaded in alternating directions for this band.

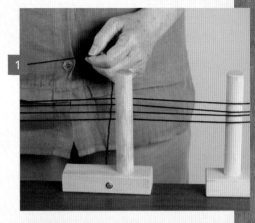

1 Place the pegs 40" (101.5 cm) apart. Tie the first color to the starting peg and run 4 warps (2 loops) in the same path, keeping them on the same side of the cross. Next, run 4 warps in the opposite path, making a cross where they intersect.

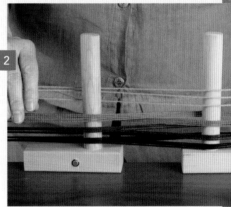

2 Change colors at the first peg by tying off the old color and tying on the new. Continue warping 4 threads of each color on each side of the cross, changing colors as you wish. With each color, remember to alternate the direction in which the warps pass through the cross and keep them in groups of 4.

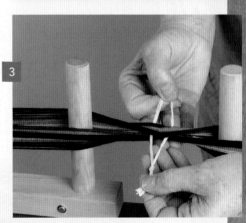

3 After all the colors you need are threaded on the warping pegs, tie the cross securely with string.

4   Tie the warp bundle together at the beginning and ending pegs.

5   Slide the entire bundle off the first peg. Chain the warp to keep the yarns from getting tangled.

6   Slip the warp bundle off the last peg. Tie the warp bundle to a peg or clamp in preparation for threading the cards.

7   Cut the end of the warp (see page 28). Holding the warp firmly in place, cut the end of the cross-tie. Slide the first group of 4 warps out of the bundle, being careful not to disturb the remaining warps.

8   Thread the first card with these 4 warps; the threads will come up through the holes from underneath the card. (All the threads on each card must pass through in the same direction or the card won't turn.)

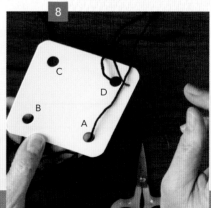

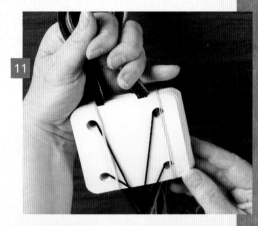

9 The next card will be threaded with the warp threads passing from the top of the card down.

10 Continue to alternate the direction of threading the cards and work through the colors as they come off the cross. Keep all the cards in order as you thread them.

11 Lay the completed stack in a bundle. Secure the cards with rubber bands.

12 Straighten the warp ends, adjusting them so they are held under even tension.

13 Tie a knot in the bundle of warps at the end. Slide the cards to the back peg.

threading direction

For cards threaded from left to right, the threads will show on the face of the cards after they pass up through the holes; for cards threaded from right to left, the threads will show on the face of the cards before they pass down through the holes.

14 Tie the ends of a piece of sturdy cord together and attach it to the back peg with a lark's head knot.

15 Tie a loose overhand knot in the other end of the bundle of warp threads and attach it to the same peg using a lark's head knot at the other end of the cord. Repeat to tie the front end of the warp to the front peg.

16 Adjust any loose warps and re-check the threading to make sure the cards are threaded alternately. The cards hang in an orientation based on their threading direction, so you can see in an instant if the cards are threaded in the correct orientation—for this band, in a series of Vs.

17 Insert a warp stick in the open shed created by the cards. Hold the pack loosely in your hand and turn the entire pack of cards one-quarter turn away from you, creating a new shed.

18 Insert a second stick in the new shed. Turn the cards one-quarter turn away from you again.

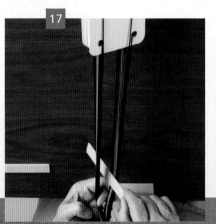

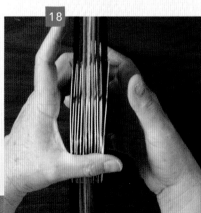

weaving

As the cards are turned in sequence, a shed is created for the weft to pass. As the cards are turned, the warps twine around each other, and the weft holds the cords together in a narrow band.

As you turn the cards, the warp length is taken up, so you will need to adjust the tension periodically to allow for tightening of the warp. On a too-tight warp, it is difficult to beat the weft in properly; there should be some give in the tension at first. As you weave and notice the tension increasing, adjust the tension.

1   To begin weaving, insert the weft.

2   Turn the cards away from you one-quarter turn. Fold the tail of the weft into the next shed. Pass the weft in the same shed. (Continue folding the tail into new sheds a few times until it is completely anchored.)

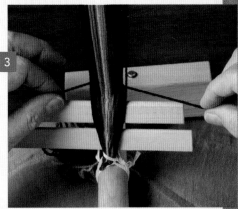

3   Tug on the wefts to ensure that they are tight against the selvedges.

4   Beat the wefts in place with your hand or the shuttle edge. Continue to pass the weft, turn the cards, and beat the weft in place.

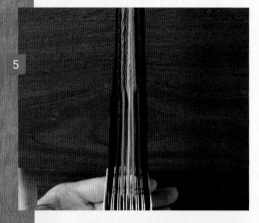

5 As you turn the cards forward and twist the warp between you and the cards, threads are also twisting beyond the cards, and this twist build-up needs to be released or it will restrict the weaving area. As you weave, periodically reverse the direction of turning the cards. Insert the weft after each turn, no matter which direction the pack is turning. You will need to do this several times in weaving this band. You can choose to space these reversals evenly by counting the rows of weaving between reversals; or just keep an eye on the twist build up at the back of the loom and reverse the direction when needed.

6 When the cards are turned back, there is an area where the warps are left on the surface, creating a noticeable bump in the band.

add weft

If you run out of weft yarn and need to add more, weave the new weft and the old together for a few shots, then drop the old and continue with the new.

7　When you are satisfied with your sample, cut the weft thread, leaving a tail. With the tail threaded on a tapestry needle, pass the weft through the last few rows of weaving, following the weft thread path.

8　Cut the band from the remaining warps, wash and press the band, and trim any weft left hanging close to the selvedge edge.

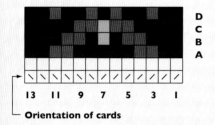

D
C
B
A

13 11 9 7 5 3 1

Orientation of cards

patterned
bands

Some bands have threaded-in patterns; we will use simple threaded-in designs. The pattern shows the color order for each card as well as the threading direction indicated. In this pattern, each vertical column represents one card. The letters on the cards indicate which hole to thread with which color.

The diagonal lines below each column indicate the direction in which the threads will be threaded through the holes. The lines show what the cards look like from the weaver's perspective when they are threaded. The cards hang at an angle, indicated by the direction of the slash mark, according to which way the threads run through them. In this pattern, the left six cards are threaded from left to right and the right seven cards are threaded from right to left. After you are finished warping, double-check to make sure the cards are oriented to match the pattern. If the pattern shows a mistake or appears to be woven upside-down, check your threading direction.

This pattern is more complex than the striped band, using several colors per card. The second sampler uses the loom instead of warp pegs to hold the yarns under tension. Set up the pegs for warping as for the striped pattern.

1 Tie the first color (red) to the starting peg and run 4 warps (2 loops) in the same path. Tie the second color (orange) to the starting peg and run 2 warps (1 loop) each of red and orange on the other side of the cross. Continue to follow the pattern, following the color order of the pattern and alternating groups of 4 warp threads on each side of the cross.

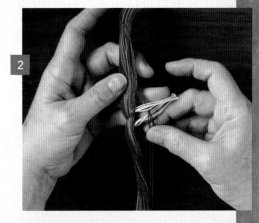

2 Attach the warp to the loom or pegs (see page 28). Cut the ties of the cross. Slide the first group of 4 warps out of the bundle, being careful not to disturb the remaining warps.

3 For this band, the cards are threaded from left to right on the left six cards and from right to left on the right seven cards. Starting at the bottom row of the pattern and threading from right to left, thread the first color in hole A, the next color in hole B, and so on for the first card.

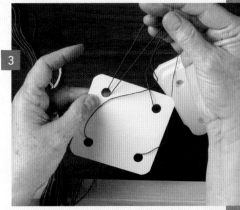

4 Continue threading the remaining cards, following the color order in the draft. Remember to change the threading direction for the second half of the cards, keeping them in order as you thread them.

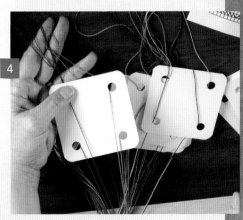

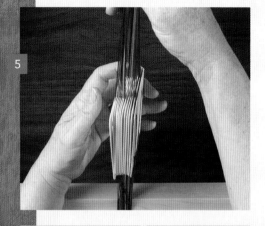

5 Holding the cards together in the order in which they were threaded, straighten the warp ends. Check that the letter orientation on the cards matches throughout (i.e., As together, Bs together, etc.).

6 Tie and wind on the warp threads to the back beam of the loom.

7 Weave as for the striped band, turning the cards forward until the twist builds up, then reversing the direction.

8 As you weave while turning the cards backward—passing the weft every time the cards rotate back one-quarter turn—the pattern changes direction.

tubular
cardweaving

Bands can be made tubular by changing the way the weft is inserted.

1 To begin, set up a warp for a band following the directions for either the striped or patterned band. Weave flat as for regular cardweaving for as long as desired.

2 To begin weaving tubularly, insert the weft from one side only. Between weft passes, bring the weft thread back under the band without inserting it into the shed.

3 Beat firmly and pull tight on the weft as you go. This will make the flat band into a tube.

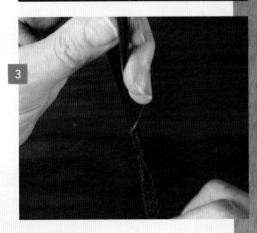

pinwheel bag

·······

for this striking bag, we will use open countered rows of soumak. Some of the wefts will travel selvedge to selvedge, while others will create pattern areas between the selvedges. While the number of warps in each sequence may vary, the thread path is always over a set number of warps, then back under fewer, and repeat.

You may wish to wrap a sampler of color choices before deciding on the final weft choices for your bag. The main design feature is in black and white, which has plenty of value contrast, so the colors shown here provide a background rather than competing with the design.

project information

yarns:
Bag—Size 10 crochet cotton (warp and hem); Tahki Cotton Classic (twining, selvedges, and soumak). Band—Tahki Cotton Classic (warp); size 10 crochet cotton (weft).

heddles:
Two 7.5- or 8-dent.

sett:
15 or 16 epi.

other materials:
Seven shuttles; hand beater; fourteen cardweaving cards; iron-on interfacing; fabric or leather trim; thin batting; button; matching sewing thread; darning needle; sewing machine; sewing needle; measuring tape.

finished measurements:
Bag fabric—about 7" (18 cm) wide and 17" (43 cm) long. Band—45" (114.5 cm) long.

soumak
fabric

The warps needed for this bag are determined by the pattern, which calls for 52 warp pairs, not the estimate of final fabric size. The length of the bag is also determined by the pattern and will vary depending on how firmly you beat the fabric. The approximate length is two squares, plus the area for the bottom of the bag.

warping math

Fabric width =
104 ends ÷ 15 epi = 7.2" (18 cm)

Finished length: About 17" (43 cm)
(94 rows of soumak)
• Add 12" (30.5 cm) for three
  samples = 29" (73.5 cm)
• Add 42" (101.5 cm) for loom
  waste, warping waste, and
  waste between samples = 71"
  (180.5 cm)

Final calculations:
104 ends x 71" (180.5 cm) for
finished fabric of about 7" (18 cm)
wide and 17" (180.5 cm) long.

warping plan

Set up the loom so that the back beam is at least 71" (180.5 cm) from the peg. Warp the loom following the directions for warping two heddles (see page 24). Wind the warp onto the back beam using sticks as packing material. Thread both heddles and secure the warp to the loom. Wind a shuttle with the crochet cotton hem yarn and weave a header. Insert sticks after the header for a firm beating surface.

weaving

Begin with a row of single-color twining (see page 58) to secure the wefts and set the spacing of the warps, then weave a ½" (1.3 cm) hem of crochet cotton. Beat the hem down tightly to cover the warp.

Begin with two rows of black open countered soumak. Use a separate shuttle for the foundation weft, each selvedge, and each color of soumak yarn. Wrap each selvedge separately to maintain the line of the weaving, and weave two shots of crochet cotton between rows of soumak.

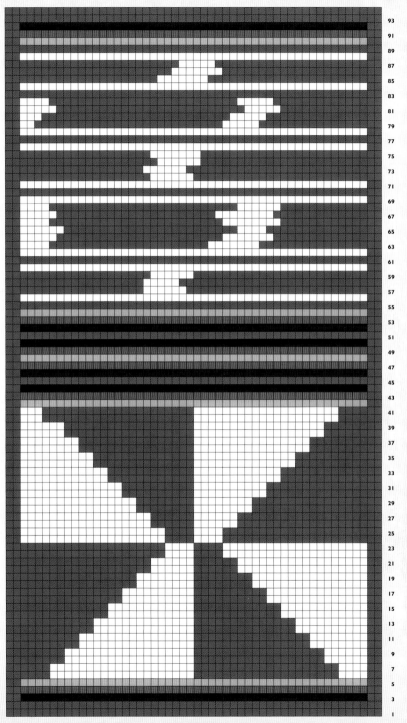

Each column on the graph represents 1 pair of warp threads, and each row represents an out-and-back soumak row. Introduce new colors as shown on the graph. On the top part of the graph, the chart may require you to pass over 2 warp threads (instead of 4) to maintain the color pattern.

There will be times when the shuttle moves from one area to another, skipping several warps. If the distance between uses of the color is short, carry the weft along the back between areas of wrapping. If the weft needs to "float" for a longer distance, add another shuttle of the same color.

Finish weaving the bag according to the chart, ending with a hem and a row of twining. Cut the fabric off the loom, then wash and dry it. (Take care to prevent the colors from running on the white area of the fabric; you may wish to add Synthrapol or a dye magnet to the wash.) Press with a warm iron.

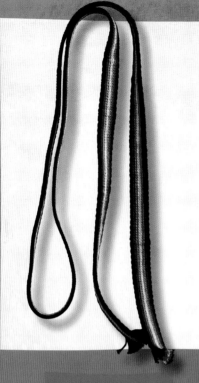

cardwoven band

The surface of one type of cardweaving mimics the surface of countered soumak—a neat trick to make a matching band for this bag.

warping plan

Setting up the pegs at least 72" (183 cm) from end to end, follow the directions on page 79 to warp the band. Wind 4 warp threads on each side of the cross (for 8 warp threads in each color) as follows: black, red, orange, melon, orange, red, black. Tie cross and ends and set up the warp on a loom, pegs, or clamps.

We will use one color in each card to make solid stripes, threading the cards in opposing directions as for the Striped Band on page 79. Threading the cards this way makes the threads twist in opposite ways and creates a surface appearance like soumak. Thread the first card with 4 black yarns passing from right to left; thread the second card with 4 black yarns passing from left to right. Repeat the sequence for each color, alternating the direction the cards are threaded with each card. Secure both ends of the warp. Start with a small header, inserting sticks to spread the warp and to have something firm to beat against.

weaving

Insert the weft, leaving a tail, and rotate the cards one-quarter turn. Beat the weft in place with your hands or shuttle and turn the cards again. Pass the tail and the shuttle in opposite directions, turn the cards, and beat. Continue to weave until the band measures 45" (114.5 cm).

When the twist builds up too much to continue weaving comfortably, turn the cards backward (reverse the direction while continuing to insert the weft at each turn) to remove some of the twist. When the band reaches the desired length, finish the weft (see page 85). Remove the band from the loom, then wash, dry, and press it.

construction

Following the directions on page 36, finish the two top edges of the pinwheel fabric with leather, fabric, or velvet, and attach the band to the center bottom of the bag. Make a lining envelope and secure it to the top edges of the bag. Sew on a button and make a button loop for the closure.

knotted cut pile

yarns:
Warp and foundation weft—crochet cotton. Soumak and selvedges—Tahki Cotton Classic. Twining and pile weft—Brown Sheep Lamb's Pride.

heddles:
Two 7.5- or 8-dent.

tools:
Three shuttles; hand beater; thread snips.

Knotted cut pile has been used for centuries for many textile applications. Rugs are the most visible pile textile represented in the West, but various types of bags, animal trappings, saddle covers, cushions, and door hangings are also commonly made using this technique. Knotted pile is still used over a widespread geographic area, from Eastern Europe, throughout Asia, North Africa, and Spain.

All of the weave structures we have learned so far will be combined with knotting to create the last three bags in the series. Pile weaving provides a rare opportunity to use a free-form graphic design in weaving. Each knot can be a different color, making design possibilities endless.

yarns

Materials for knotted pile include wools of all types, silk, and more recently cotton. Any animal fiber, from sheep's wool to camel and goat hair has been spun and used for all facets of this weave structure. Silk has been used for the entire textile and in conjunction with wools as pile only. Cotton is generally reserved for warp and foundation weft, not pile.

There are six weaving functions to consider in choosing yarns needed for a pile construction: warp, pile knotting yarn, foundation weft, selvedge weft, twining weft, and soumak weft. The bags use the same yarn for warp and foundation weft, a second yarn for selvedge weft, twining, and soumak weft, and another for the pile, for a total of three different yarns for each bag.

Crochet cotton works perfectly for warp: it holds the tight tension needed and resists abrasion. It also works as a fine foundation weft, being flexible enough to undulate around the warps as necessary, strong enough to hold everything together, and subtle enough to visually disappear under the pile knots. The foundation (or ground) weft creates the structure of the textile; the warp and foundation weft form the canvas on which the knots will hang. The foundation weft bears equal burden with the warp for the integrity of the textile. It needs to be hard wearing—your textile is only as durable as your yarns.

There are two primary considerations when trying out a yarn for pile: how many knots per inch to use and how the colors work together. Ideally, a design will square—that is, it will have as many vertical rows per inch as linear knots per inch. I tried a different pile weft on each bag, adjusting the number of strands used to keep the sett constant. The pile yarns come in a grand variety of colors; the projects can be personalized by color choices of your own.

Pile wefts are meant to open up (or bloom) once cut to create their velvet surface. For commercial rugs, time is saved by not plying, but for my work, I have found it easier to dye and manipulate plied yarns. The pile yarn is also used as twining at the beginning and end of each piece, to set the spacing for the pile knots.

The final yarns chosen for each project are selvedge and soumak yarn, which vary depending on the pile weft yarn.

To check that a yarn or bundle of yarns is appropriate for pile weaving on your sett, fold the yarn(s) in half and insert a length between warp yarns. The folded bundle should not deflect the warps yarns; it should fit neatly and fill the space without crowding.

This yarn is too big to weave in this sett; it deflects the warp threads.

pile knots

Knotting is a misnomer—we are actually wrapping the yarn around contiguous warps to create the pile structure we know as knotted cut pile. The symmetrical knot is commonly used by tribal weavers for the coarser durable everyday textiles made for personal use.

It is a secure structure, leaving two ends to emerge together from the center beneath the bar created by the knot. We will tie this symmetrical knot on two contiguous warps held taut and flat. The knotting process is not difficult, requiring only the simplest of looms and a few tools. We will be using the rigid-heddle loom, and making small pieces, but the methods and tools presented here can be expanded and adapted later using other types of looms or for making larger textiles.

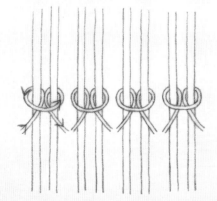

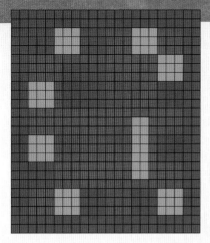

reading a pile pattern

Each square in the chart represents a single knot tied over 2 warp threads. This chart indicates 22 knots in each row, or 44 warp ends overall. The pattern at right creates the sample at left.

Sample pile pattern

warp and
weave hem

Before the pile section, begin with a header, twining, a plain-weave hem, and a row of countered soumak.

Following the directions for single-peg double-heddle warping (see page 24), set up the loom so that the peg is about 40" (101.5 cm) in front of the back beam. Warp two 8-dent heddles with 52 ends. The leftmost thread should be in a slot so that the foundation weft exits toward the back and does not get cut as you cut the pile knots. Make sure the warp is evenly tensioned and held taut. Weave a header to establish the width of the warp, then insert sticks for a firm beating surface (see page 32).

1 Wind one shuttle with crochet cotton for the foundation weft and two more with Tahki Cotton Classic for the soumak and selvedges. With the pile weft yarn, work a row of single twining. With crochet cotton, work a short hem. With Cotton Classic, work a row of open countered soumak, wrapping the selvedges separately.

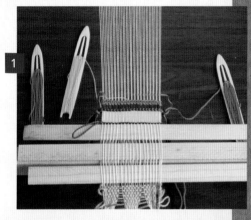

2 Pass the foundation weft back and forth, beating in place.

knotted pile

1 Starting at the left side, skip the first 4 warps (the selvedge) and pick up the fifth and sixth warps.

2 Pass the cut end of the pile yarn between these 2 warps from front to back, behind, and around the left-hand warp.

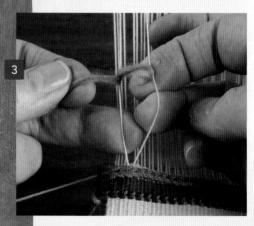

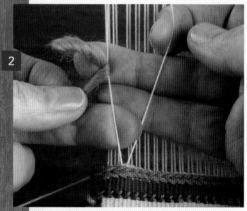

3 Wrap the pile yarn over both warps above the pile yarn, around the right-hand warp of the pair, back under, and out in the same location as the beginning yarn.

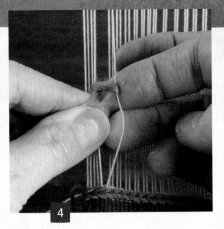

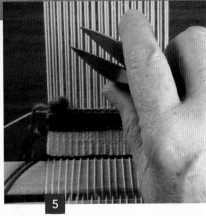

4 Grasp the 2 tail ends and pull the knot down to the fell line.

5 Trim to about ¼" (6 mm). Including the knot, the depth to the warps will be about ⅜" (1 cm).

6 After tying the knots in the row (omitting the selvedge warp threads), wrap the selvedges in a figure eight as for soumak until the yarn is level with the row of knots or slightly above. (The number of wraps will change with the yarns you are using, from one wrap to several.)

7 With the heddle, open a shed. Pass the foundation weft from left to right; this straight row helps maintain the width of the piece. Hold it firmly as it is beaten in.

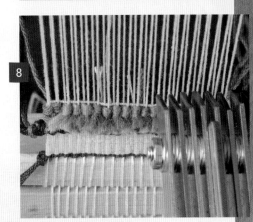

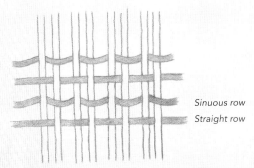

Sinuous row
Straight row

8 Beat using the hand beater, taking care not to pull in on the left side.

9 Change the shed and pass the foundation weft from right to left; leave plenty of extra weft in the second pass to allow the yarn to circumnavigate the warps. This sinuous row helps maintain the height of the work. Beat with a flicking motion in the open shed to help place the weft in properly. Return the heddle to the resting position and begin a new row of knots.

10 To change colors in knotted pile, either work across knot by knot or make all the knots in one color before changing to a new color.

11 Continue working until all the rows are complete and end with one or two rows of open countered soumak.

sample

There will be some draw-in at the beginning of any weaving, so use the beginning of the warp to sample colors as you set the weaving width. Colors in knotted pile are hard to imagine from the skein. When we look at yarn, we are looking at the side of the spun yarn, but in knotted cut pile, we see the cut end of the yarn. You can take a sample of your proposed yarns and bundle a few cut ends to see how they will work together (below right).

The best test is a woven color sample. Colors of the same value that are close in hue will not show as separate colors, obscuring the design. Better to find that out at the beginning and change colors if needed than regret your color choices in the finished textile.

troubleshooting

There is ancient thought that we should make an intentional mistake in our work so as not to offend the gods. There is no need, in knotted cut pile, to make a mistake intentionally—most likely you will make one unintentionally. Correct a problem when you can, move on when you can't. Do not let a mistake paralyze you or prevent you from finishing your work. The following fixes address common errors in knotted pile.

Use sticks to shim an uneven warp.

uneven warp tension

Some problems that arise with pile weaving are due to tension issues of the warp. Be sure, when winding the warp, that it is as even as possible. As you are weaving, you may notice the fell line is uneven, either with a bow or dip in the center or a dip to one side. In an area of loose tension, the knots do not beat down as well and that area bows up. It is possible to shim loose warps. If some parts of the warp are looser than others, place a stick or two between the warp and back beam to tighten those areas.

uneven edges

Measure frequently to make sure the warp maintains its width. Don't attempt to reestablish the width all at once; the process has to be gradual. If it is bowing out, there are a few options to try:

- Use the first pass (straight pass) of the foundation weft to pull in the left side.
- Use the second pass (sinuous pass) of the foundation weft to pull in the right side.
- Work a row or more of twining instead of two passes of the foundation weft if the bowing is particularly severe.

If the edges of the piece are pulling in, try one of the following:

- Tie a cord from each side of the piece, just below the fell line, to the side of the loom. This should help pull the selvedge back into place.
- Make sure the foundation weft is not too tight in either direction (without leaving loops at the edges as you correct the selvedges).

knotting errors

If you find you have woven an incorrect color in a pattern sequence, you can pull out a knot (even several rows down) and re-insert it with a needle.

1 Using the needle, move the foundation weft to allow access to the knot you want to replace.

2 Remove the misplaced knot, leaving 2 exposed warp threads.

3 With the correct yarn threaded on a tapestry needle, wrap the 2 exposed threads with the pile yarn.

4 Trim the knot flush with the fell line and use the hand beater to press the wefts back in place.

distorted pattern

The diagrams for the bags assume that the pile knots are square—that is, that the number of knots in an inch is the same whether measured in vertical rows or in linear wrapped warps. Before making this sampler, I tried one with a sett of 12 epi, using the same yarns. The sett was too far apart, causing the squares to stretch horizontally. If the proportions of your project aren't coming out like you envisioned, try one of the following changes:

- Change the sett; use more ends per inch for a narrower design and fewer for a wider one.
- Use thicker or thinner pile yarn.
- Use thicker or thinner warp yarn.
- Hold several yarns together for the cut pile (known as stranding).
- Change the foundation weft.

Weaving the same pattern at 12 epi instead of 16 epi stretched the pattern out of proportion.

finishing
cut pile

Wash the pile pieces like the other projects (in hot water and detergent; see page 35), but instead of ironing, lay them flat on a towel to dry completely. Trim any ends that are left hanging, fluff the pile sections (I use a hairbrush), and trim all fringe edges.

travel bag

project information

yarns:
Bag—crochet cotton (warp and foundation weft); Vevgarn (pile weft and twining), Davidson's Navaho Warp (selvedges and soumak). Bands—Tahki Cotton Classic (warp); crochet cotton (weft).

heddles:
Two 7.5- or 8-dent.

sett:
15 or 16 epi.

other materials:
Three shuttles; hand beater; thread snips; fifteen cardweaving cards; sewing machine; matching sewing thread; linen or other bag fabric; iron-on interfacing; lining fabric.

finished measurements:
Fabric bag: 14" x 10¾" x 5" (35.5 x 27.5 x 12.5 cm). Woven pockets: two 5½" × 6½" (14 x 16.5 cm) pieces. Cardwoven bands: Two bands, each 1¼" x 50" (3.2 x 127 cm).

it was important to me that all of the bags in this book be functional; one of my most useful bags is my travel bag. It holds my travel documents in the pockets, my glasses, some knitting, a book or magazine, and anything else I might need should I be delayed or find myself without my checked luggage in some strange hotel. I designed a simple version using two pockets of wool pile, a commercial linen fabric for the bag, and cardwoven handles.

Each of the pile pockets is inspired by a view from an airplane window. The bands were inspired by a student in one of my bandweaving classes (see page 134).

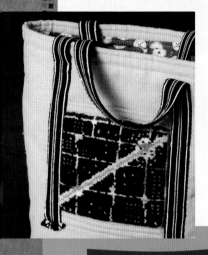

pile fabric

The first pile weaving project features two simple squares sewn as pockets on a commercial-fabric bag. The pockets will be plush and very durable.

warping plan

Set up the loom so that the back beam is at least 60" (152.5 cm) from the peg. Warp the loom following the directions for warping two heddles (see page 24). Wind the warp onto the back beam using sticks as packing material. Thread the second heddle and secure the warp to the loom. Wind a shuttle with the crochet cotton hem yarn and weave a header. Insert sticks after the header. Wind a shuttle of crochet cotton and two of Navaho warp.

weaving

With 2 strands of Vevgarn, work a row of twining to spread the warp. With crochet cotton, weave a short hem. With Navaho warp, work a row of open countered soumak. Use the hand beater to press the wefts firmly in place. Work small areas of your intended colors in various combinations to see how they work together, passing the foundation weft (crochet cotton) between each row of knots. Finish the sample with another row of soumak, short hem, and row of twining. Insert three or four sticks (about 3" [7.5 cm]) in the sheds after each sample to leave enough room to cut them apart.

Begin the first pocket with a row of twining using 2 strands of Vevgarn. With crochet cotton, weave a small hem. With Navaho Warp, weave a row of open countered soumak, wrapping the selvedges individually.

Following the Night Sky chart, begin the knotted pile section of the first pocket. After each row of knotted pile, pass the foundation weft and wrap the selvedges. It will usually require two turns of Navaho Warp yarn to keep the selvedges even with the pile, though one turn may be enough. Adjust according to the needs of the fabric.

When the Night Sky chart is complete, work a row of open countered soumak with Navaho Warp. Weave a short hem with crochet cotton and work a row of twining with Vevgarn.

Weave a few inches with waste yarn between the two panels or insert more sticks, then begin the second panel. Work the second pocket like the first—work a row of twining, weave a hem, work one row of open countered soumak, follow the Farm in Winter chart, then finish with soumak, plain weave, and twining.

Cut the fabric off the loom, cut the samples and pockets apart, then wash the pockets in hot water with a little detergent. Soak in clear water to rinse and lay them flat to dry overnight. Once they are fully dry, trim any errant yarn that has popped up.

Night Sky

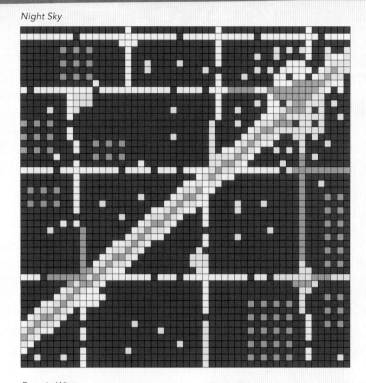

Farm in Winter

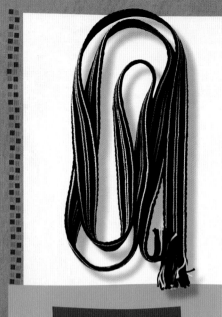

cardwoven
bands

At first I made a plain-weave band for this bag, but the cardwoven version is thicker, stronger, wider, and more durable for hard use.

Setting up the pegs at least 144" (366 cm) from end to end, follow the directions on pages 78–84 to prepare to warp the band. Wind the warp threads in groups of four, alternating sides of the cross, as follows: 4 black, 4 white, 16 black, 4 yellow, 4 black, 4 yellow, 16 black, 4 white, 4 black. (Each card is 4 ends, so there will be 44 ends of black and 8 each of yellow and white.)

Tie cross and ends and set up the warp on a loom, pegs, or clamps. Thread the cards in alternating directions. Thread the first card with 4 black yarns passing from right to left; thread the second card with 4 white yarns passing from left to right. Repeat for the remaining 13 cards, alternating the direction the cards are threaded with each card. Secure both ends of the warp. Start with a small header, inserting sticks to spread the warp and to have something firm to beat against.

Wind a shuttle with size 10 black crochet cotton weft.

weaving

Insert the weft, leaving a tail, and rotate the cards one-quarter turn away from you. Beat the weft in place with your hands or shuttle. Pass the tail and the shuttle in opposite directions, turn the cards, and beat. Continue to weave until the band measures 50" (127 cm), then finish the weft with a needle. Work about an inch of waste yarn and weave the second band the same length.

warping math

Finished width:
60 ends = 15 cards

Finished length:
2 bands, each 50" (127 cm) = 100" (254 cm).
- Add 20% (20" [51 cm]) for take-up and shrinkage = 120" (305 cm)
- Add 24" (61 cm) for loom and warping waste = 144" (366 cm)

Final calculations:
60 ends x 144" (366 cm) for two finished bands 1¼" (3.2 cm) wide and 50" (127 cm) long.

When the twist builds up too much to continue weaving comfortably, turn the cards backward to remove some of the twist while continuing to insert the weft, beating each time. When the band reaches the desired length, finish the weft (see page 85). Remove the band from the loom, cut between the two bands, then wash, dry, and press it. (If you prefer a handbag rather than a shoulder bag, weave the handles shorter.)

construction

Cut a piece of linen to 40" × 18" (101.5 × 45.5 cm) for the body. Cut 2 pockets from the remaining linen, each 2" (5 cm) longer and 1" (2.5 cm) wider than the pile pieces. Cut a 40" × 18" (101.5 × 45.5 cm) piece of lining fabric and a matching piece of interfacing. Cut a piece of lining fabric 6" × 6½" (15 × 16.5 cm) for the interior pocket. Iron the interfacing to the wrong side of the body fabric, following the manufacturer's instructions. Fold the body in half and mark the midpoint of each side with a pin.

pile pockets

Make the pockets, which are linen (or bag fabric) with the woven panels sewn on the front. Trim the excess warps close to the twining edge. The top and bottom edges of each pocket will be the right side of the linen. Place one cut-pile patch centered face-up on the wrong side of one piece of linen. Fold the top and bottom of the linen ½", then fold over again to cover over the hems of the patch. Topstitch close to the soumak edge of the patch. Handstitch the selvedge edges of the pile panel to the linen. Repeat for the second panel (see Fig. 1).

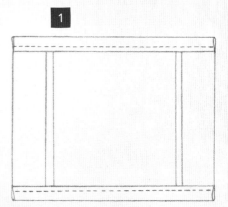

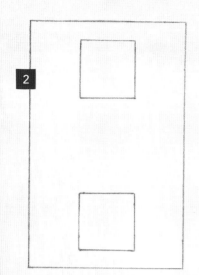

2

attach pile pockets and handles

With the right side of the body fabric facing, place the pockets on the body fabric about 5" (12.5 cm) from the top and bottom and pin in place (see Fig. 2). (Remember to position the second pocket upside-down so that it will be oriented correctly when the side seams are sewn.) Stitch the sides of the pockets in place. Stitch along the bottom edge of each pocket through all layers.

Lay the fabric flat with the right side facing up and pin one handle in place along each side of one pile pocket of the fabric; repeat with other handle and pocket. Sew the handles in place with top stitches, reinforcing as needed, to 3" (7.5 cm) from the ends of the fabric. (The top edges will be turned down and stitched once the sides are sewn in place.)

inside pocket

Press the edges of the inside pocket piece ¼" (6 mm) to the wrong side on all sides. Press under the top edge 1" (2.5 cm) and stitch to hem. With wrong side of lining fabric facing, iron interfacing to wrong side of lining fabric to correspond with inside pocket location. With lining fabric and pocket right side up, stitch pocket in place along sides and bottom.

assemble

The rest of the bag is worked for the Project Bag (see page 43). With the wrong sides of the lining fabric and woven fabric held together and the batting sandwiched between, sew the lining to the woven fabric around all the edges with zigzag or straight stitches. The lining and bag fabric will be handled as one piece from now on.

With the right side of the lining facing out, sew the side seams of the bag (see Fig.3). Fold and sew triangle gussets (see page 38) to shape the bottom, making the bottom of the bag 5" (12.5 cm) wide. Fold over the top edge 1" (2.5 cm) twice and topstitch at least two rows around the top edge.

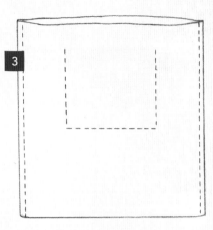

textile
traditions

·········

this is the most traditionally inspired design of the bag. The front of the bag is woven in sunny golds and warm reds, which evoke the naturally dyed colors of antique textiles from all over Central Asia. This sun sign, an almost universal symbol, is a balanced composition typical of indigenous designs: all four quarters of the design are the same, just rotated. The pattern is progressive: one row leads to another in a geometric progression.

The same colors make up the back of the bag, which appears to be a textile fragment. Since these textiles take precious time and materials to construct, it is common for weavers to use fragments of these old rugs and bags in a new application.

project information

yarns:
Bag—crochet cotton (warp and foundation weft); Paternayan (pile and soumak), Davidson's Navaho Warp (selvedges, soumak, and twining). Band—Tahki Cotton Classic (warp); crochet cotton (weft).

heddles:
Two 7.5- or 8-dent.

sett:
15 or 16 epi.

other materials:
Five shuttles; hand beater; fourteen cardweaving cards; thread snips; measuring tape; sewing machine; matching sewing thread; lining fabric; batting; leather, velvet, or other trim fabric; darning needle; button.

finished measurements:
Bag—7½" x 6½" x 1" (19 x 16.5 x 2.5 cm).
Band—50" (127 cm) long x 1" (2.5 cm) wide.

pile
fabric

The pile in this bag is Paternayan needlepoint yarn, which is comprised of three strands of two-ply yarns, making for six plies in the final construction. The yarn is particularly suitable for rug weaving because it is composed of longwool fibers, which are durable and lustrous. The unique yarn construction coupled with the wide color selection allows for an incredible range of color-stranding possibilities, a big advantage when trying to find specific colors using commercially available yarns. (Stranding is holding two or more colors together and using them as if they are one yarn; see page 130 for more details on using the technique.)

see page 130

warping math

Fabric width:
118 ends (55 knots + 8 selvedge ends) = about 6½" (16.5 cm)

Finished length:
about 18" (45.5 cm) long (111 rows pile + 2" (5 cm) soumak bottom + hems)
• Add 12" (30.5 cm) for three samples = 30" (76 cm)
• Add 30" (76 cm) for loom waste, warping waste, and waste between samples = 60" (152.5 cm)

Final calculations:
118 ends x 60" (152.5 cm) for finished fabric of about 6½" (16.5 cm) wide and 18" (45.5 cm) long.

warping plan

Set up the loom so that the back beam is at least 60" (152.5 cm) from the peg. Warp the loom following the directions for warping two heddles (see page 24). Wind the warp onto the back beam using sticks as packing material. Thread the second heddle and secure the warp to the loom. Wind a shuttle with the crochet cotton hem yarn and weave a header. Insert three sticks after the header. Wind two shuttles with Navaho Warp, and one with Paternayan in red.

see page 24

weaving

To spread the warp, work a sampler with twining, a hem, soumak, and figure-eight selvedges. Try the pile yarns you plan to use, stranding them in different combinations to help decide which you like best. Finish the sampler with soumak, a hem, and twining. Insert two sticks before beginning the project (see page 32).

With Navaho Warp, work a row of twining. With crochet cotton, work a ½" (1.3 cm) hem. With Navaho Warp, work a row of open countered soumak.

see page 32

placket

To leave space for a closure at the top of the bag, weave a placket of red yarn in an extended diamond pattern. Wind a shuttle with Paternayan red and start the new weft at the left side (after the selvedges), leaving a tail hanging. With the shed closed, pass the new weft over and under pairs of warps following the Placket chart.

Where the chart shows one or more red squares, bring the shuttle above the warp and pass over as many warp pairs as there are red squares. Where the chart shows one or more white squares, bring the shuttle to the back of the warp and pass under as many warp pairs as there are white squares.

After the first row is complete, wrap the selvedges. With the shed open, fold in the tail of the new yarn before passing the foundation weft once; change the shed and pass the foundation weft again. Carry the pattern shuttle over and under warps according to the graph and following each pattern row with the selvedge wraps and two shots

of foundation weft. Finish with a row of countered soumak with Navaho Warp.

pile

Follow the Sun chart and the directions on pages 99–102; continue to wrap the selvedges separately (about two figure eights per row) and pass the foundation weft after each row of knots.

At the end of the Sun chart, work 1 row open countered soumak with Navaho warp, 13 rows with red Paternayan, and 1 row with Navaho warp, passing the foundation weft between rows. Wrap each selvedge 3 times per row of soumak; adjust as needed to keep the row even. At the end of the soumak portion, work the Carpet chart. Work 1 row soumak with Navaho Warp and repeat the Placket. Finish with a row of soumak, a crochet cotton hem, and twining.

Cut the bag from the loom. Wash it in hot water with detergent, soak in hot water to rinse, and lay flat to dry.

Carpet chart

Sun chart

band

Although I originally imagined a band made with a traditional pick-up technique, a plainer cardwoven band complemented the pile without overwhelming it. The band has four colors of red Cotton Classic threaded randomly for a mottled look. It is substantial enough to hold up to hard use, the colors work with the wool of the pile, and the band does not compete with the graphic image on the bag faces.

warping plan

Setting up the pegs at least 80" (203 cm) from end to end, follow the directions on pages 79–84 to warp the band. Use up to 4 shades of red in Tahki Cotton Classic for this band, arranged randomly. Wind 4 warp threads on each side of the cross. Tie end cross and ends and set up the warp on a loom, pegs, or clamps.

Thread the cards in alternating directions with the colors in random order. Secure both ends of the warp. Start with a small header, inserting sticks to spread the warp and to have something firm to beat against.

weaving

Insert the weft, leaving a tail, and rotate the cards one-quarter turn. Beat the weft in place with your hands or shuttle. Pass the tail and the shuttle in opposite directions, turn the cards, and beat. Continue to weave until the band measures 50" (127 cm).

When the twist builds up too much to continue weaving comfortably, reverse the turning direction as you continue to weave to remove some of the twist. When the band reaches the desired length, finish the weft (see page 85). Remove the band from the loom, then wash, dry, and press it.

warping math

Finished width:
  56 ends = 1" (2.5 cm)

Finished length: 50" (127 cm)
  • Add 20% (10" [25.5 cm]) for take-up and shrinkage = 60" (152.5 cm)
  • Add 20" for loom and warping waste = 80" (203 cm)

Final calculations:
  56 ends x 80" (203 cm) for a finished band 1" (2.5 cm) wide and 50" (127 cm) long

construction

Following the directions for the First Bag (see pages 35–39), finish the top edge of each end of the fabric, leaving the plackets exposed. Attach the band to the center bottom and along the side of the bag.

Make an envelope lining and square the bottom corners. Insert lining and interlining of quilt batting, if desired.

Sew button to the Sun side of the bag and make a buttonhole closure.

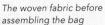

The woven fabric before assembling the bag

spiral
star

·········

this colorful bag has bold contemporary imagery which contrasts with the traditional techniques used in its construction. The reeled silk used in the pile makes this a fine choice for an evening bag, and its small size makes it easy to carry. The spiral design expresses cyclical movement in cheerful colors, bordered with simple elements.

This silk bag is comprised of one piece of fabric, wholly woven on the rigid-heddle loom. The warp for the pile area is still cotton, as is the foundation weft, making a sturdy under-structure for the pile knots. Soumak makes up the area under the flap, giving an additional area for patterning if desired.

project information

yarns:
Bag—crochet cotton (warp and foundation weft); reeled silk, sizes 0 and 8/2 (pile, selvedges, and soumak). Band—Reeled silk, size 8/2.

heddles:
Two 7.5- or 8-dent.

sett:
15 or 16 epi.

other materials:
Four shuttles; hand beater; thread snips; sewing machine; matching thread; lining fabric; velvet, or other fabric for trim and lining band; batting; darning needle; one button.

finished measurements:
Bag—7¼" x 8¼" x 1" (18.5 cm x 21 x 2.5 cm). Band—1" (2.5 cm) wide and 54" (137 cm) long.

pile fabric

Silk is the most luxurious of fibers used to weave pile fabrics. It does not felt, which among luxury fibers is unusual, and its luster, ability to reflect light and take dye makes it stand out like no other fiber. Pile uses surprisingly small amounts of fiber, making the expense of a silk bag less of a consideration than it would be with other silk textiles.

warping math

Fabric width:
130 ends (61 knots + 8 selvedge ends) = about 7¼" (18.5 cm).

Finished length:
About 25" (63.5cm) long (132 rows pile + 1½" (3.8 cm) soumak at top fold + soumak bottom + soumak area under flap + hems)
• Add 10" (25.5 cm) for samples = 35" (89 cm)
• Add 25" (63.5 cm) for loom waste, warping waste, and waste between samples = 60" (152.5 cm)

Final calculations:
130 ends x 60" (152.5 cm) for finished fabric of about 7¼" (18.5 cm) wide and 18" (45.5 cm) long.

warping plan

Set up the loom so that the back beam is at least 60" (152.5 cm) from the peg. Warp the loom following the directions for warping two heddles (see page 24). You will thread 4 threads in 32.5 slots, so the back heddle will have an extra pair of warps. (For the last two warps, thread one through the hole and the other through the slot in the back heddle, and thread both through the corresponding slot in the front heddle.) Mark the center of your heddle and begin threading from 16 slots to the left of center.

Wind the warp onto the back beam using sticks as packing material. Thread the second heddle and secure the warp to the loom. Wind a shuttle with the crochet cotton hem yarn and weave a header. Insert sticks after the header. Wind 3 strands of yellow silk onto each of two shuttles for selvedges.

sample

With crochet cotton, weave a header. With a triple strand of silk, work a row of twining, followed by a crochet-cotton hem. With silk, work a row of open countered soumak, then use the beginning of the warp for some color sampling. Wrap the selvedges on each row with silk until the level of the selvedges is even with the knots. Finish the sample area with soumak and twining, insert two sticks to leave space for cutting, then begin the bag.

Star chart

bag

Work twining with silk, a ½" (1.3 cm) hem with crochet cotton, and one row of open countered soumak.

Begin working pile following the Spiral chart and the directions on pages 100–103; wrap the selvedges separately and pass the foundation weft after each row of knots. At the end of the Spiral chart, work 12 rows of soumak (about 1½" [1.3 cm]) in yellow silk for the top of the bag flap, passing the foundation weft between rows. Wrap the selvedges separately as needed to keep the work even. Work the Star chart, which appears upside-down as you work it but will be right side up when the bag is assembled.

Once the pile areas are both completed, wind one shuttle with 3 strands of blue silk and another with 3 strands of red silk. With blue, work 10 rows of open countered soumak for the bottom of the bag, then begin the area that will be under the flap once the bag is constructed. You may wish to add a more graphic design here; I simply changed colors when I ran out of the blue, then again after I ran out of red. Continue wrapping the selvedges separately and passing the foundation weft after each row.

Weave a ½" (1.3 cm) hem in crochet cotton, then work a row of twining in silk. Cut the fabric off the loom, wash, and lay flat to dry. Trim any errant pile yarns.

Spiral chart

band

The band is also woven of silk in a pick-up pattern. Because the pattern involves a few rows of floats and the smooth silk catches easily, it will be lined on the wrong side for durability.

Following the directions for warping a pick-up band (see page 48), set up the loom so that the back beam is at least 74" from the peg. Follow the draft below for color placement and number of warps. Use a doubled warp for the pattern threads as for the pick-up sampler, threading 2 gold, 1 blue, and 3 gold plain-weave pairs at the border, then 7 pattern threads alternating with 6 pairs of plain weave, then the remaining border threads, for 50 threads total.

Wind the warp using paper, sticks, or corrugated cardboard for packing. Wind a shuttle with the weft yarn and weave a header.

weaving

Lock in the end of the weft thread on the first shot and weave a few inches to establish the width; this section will be cut off later. Following the chart below left, weave the band pattern for 54" (137 cm).

With a tapestry or sewing needle, pass the weft end along the weft thread of the last several rows of weaving to lock in the weft thread. Cut the band from the loom. Secure the weft threads with a needle. Wash the fabric, dry it, and press flat with a warm iron.

warping math

Finished width:
50 ends = ¾" (2 cm)

Finished length: 54" (137 cm)
• Add 20" (51 cm) for loom waste, warping waste, and take-up = 74" (188 cm)

Final calculations:
49 ends x 74" (188 cm) for a finished band ¾" (2 cm) wide and 54" (137 cm) long.

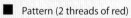

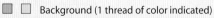

■ Pattern (2 threads of red)

■ ■ ▫ Background (1 thread of color indicated)

□ Pattern area

⊙ Pattern thread dropped down

■ Pattern thread on surface

■ ▫ Background thread on surface

construction

Following the directions on page 36, cover each end of the bag with trim fabric and batting. Fold the spiral pile section over the soumak portion (see Fig. 1 and Fig. 2) to determine where the top and bottom of the bag will be and mark the bottom with a pin on each side.

Cut a length of velvet as long as the band and ¾" (2 cm) wider. Fold under the sides of the velvet ⅜" (1 cm) and stitch along each edge ¼" (6 mm) from the fold. Center the band on the wrong side of the velvet, pin in place, and sew the band to the velvet.

Sew the band into the bottom and sides of the fabric (see page 37), leaving the spiral flap portion free. Reinforce the top edges. With lining fabric, interfacing, and batting, make an envelope lining and sew it inside the bag.

Sew the button to the trim on the soumak area under the flap. Make a buttonhole loop on the inside back of the bag for closure.

1

Wrong side of spiral

Wrong side of star

Wrong side of soumak

2

Wrong side of spiral

Soumak

design
notebook

· · · · · · · ·

Every craft requires practice and repetition to develop the necessary hand and finger movements, and it makes sense to practice on projects that are planned for you. Once you feel comfortable with the techniques, it's time to make your own decisions—to plan and execute your own projects.

beginning creatively

There is no exact recipe for creativity, but in time you will discover your own style. Your personal story, the message you wish to weave, and your history and surroundings are all rich sources of inspiration for work that you do from your heart, from your life—meaningful work that you create and no one else can.

start with what you know

Observation is a subtle brain activity; we see things all the time without really noticing them. Once you really look at something, the details that are important to you will become apparent. You always put yourself into your work, whether it is by color choices, image choices, project parameters, fiber choices, or by what you leave out. Make those choices for yourself; make what you like, not what others expect. If you create for yourself, appreciation from others will follow. When you create your pattern, or even if you use a pattern I have provided, allow yourself the luxury of changing your mind as you weave.

creativity does not happen unless you are working

Ideas are not created in a vacuum; they don't float around in the air waiting for someone to capture them. As you work, ideas flow. Ideas build on each other like bricks: learning a technique, building on tradition, your hands and mind work together to make something new. In the beginning, most works will not take your breath away, but they will be the stepping-stones to superlative work.

don't despair at mistakes

If you don't like the way something is turning out, take it out, change your plan, or use the piece as a sample and make another. Don't stop because the first project is not perfect. Mastery comes with time and practice, so jump right back in and make another. Be adventurous, try out combinations, make mistakes. It's only weaving.

there is no need to explain

We often seem to feel the need to explain our work and all the nuances that make up the process by which we arrived at the finished piece. But it is not necessary to explain yourself to anyone. People will see what they want and need to; you need not make them see what you see (unless you want to).

color

Color is ubiquitous in our world. We often see color first as an automatic response. We react emotionally to color, in both subtle and overt ways. Color means different things to different people, so you must decide what it means to you.

Color can be one of the hardest parts of designing for new weavers. If you like a certain color or series of colors—you gravitate toward them or find yourself buying clothing in a specific color range—start there. Add colors that go with the color you like, whether to complement or to contrast. If you use colors that you like, you are more likely to like what you make. Practice with simple projects, such as the series of First Bags. Get to know which colors suit you, which colors you like to see together.

It helps to make your own color wheel of yarns. It can be easier to see color subtleties and undertones when the yarns are placed next to each other and you can see how they relate to each other. You don't have to use all of the colors; choose which you like. Vary the intensity of the colors.

Train your eyes to see more than the dominant colors around you. Look carefully at things you see every day; some of the colors might surprise you. Take a color photo so you can examine the colors from one step removed.

A color wheel made of yarns shows the way the colors relate to each other.

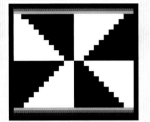 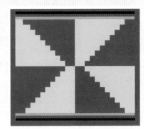 

Changing black to gray brings the colors closer into focus, because the colors and gray are the same value. Reducing the value variation of the pinwheel image highlights the colors (which are very close to each other in value). Other designs are not as dramatic in value variations, but value still plays an important part in focusing our attention.

value

Color and value set the tone and feeling: the greater the contrast in color and value, the bolder the image appears, while quiet pieces need less variation in color and value. Value variations can highlight and focus our attention to the parts of an image we wish to emphasize.

Value is the variation of the amount of white or gray in a color. It is useful in directing the viewer's eye where you want it and in setting a mood. The feeling of a piece can be accentuated by choosing high contrast for strength and dramatic attention, low contrast for calmness and quiet. Black and white is the most dramatic representation of variations in value. Strong contrast between black and white in a design will focus the viewer's attention. The main design feature of the Pinwheel Bag is in black and white, which provides plenty of value contrast. I wanted the colors to provide a background, not compete with the design. I decided on accent colors with similar value that were steps on the color scale (analogous). If the colors had more value variation, the viewer's eye would bounce between the colors and the design.

Outlines of dark or lighter colors are used to emphasize areas in a design and can make a stronger statement than the simple design itself.

 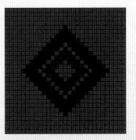 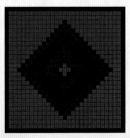

For the Sampler Star bag, I used four different yarn types for the pile: The outer border is five colors of Paternayan stranded together to make one pile yarn. Inside this border is a blend of two colors of Vevgarn, and the red background is two strands of different reds in Brown Sheep Lamb's Pride. The star itself is made up of five strands of reeled silk held together as one.

stranding

Weavers of knotted pile have unique opportunities when just the right color is not available; blending colors knot by knot or stranding several yarns together are ways to visually create the color you need. By knotting several closely related colors or holding several strands of different colors together, you can create the subtle shades and range of colors available to painters. (Although this technique is easiest to see in cut pile, you can blend yarns in other techniques, too.) You can even try other yarn sources; do not limit yourself to one line, one yarn company, or even one fiber.

Blends of colors close in value make for a richer color experience, as the various colors visually merge. Scale matters; your eye can blend colors better in small yarns than large ones.

Stranding several yellow yarns creates different color effects in soumak.

Three different ways to blend color and value: at left, by stranding the colors in the yarn (Paternayan); at center, combining stranding and knot-by-knot (Vevgarn); and at right, working knot by knot (Brown Sheep).

The eye blends the warp and weft colors more completely in the finer yarn (left) than the heavier one (right).

color inspirations

Different parts of the world express color in varying ways: hot colors of countries closer to the equator, cool colors from countries in the north. Find inspiration in other cultures; we are not bound by their traditions and expectations, but we can be inspired by them. Movies, photographs, memories, and artifacts are all full of color correspondences. A photo, even in black and white, can inspire memories you can use as colors or images in your work. Word association is a useful tool when choosing colors. Words can evoke a memory and related colors.

You do not have to be tied to reality in your color choices. Take liberties with established ideas, change things around a bit. Color changes can make a big difference in how your design is perceived. The challenge with choosing colors is where to start, how to narrow down the choices. Find an idea or a system of correspondence that you like, and begin there.

The groups of colors here represent the elements of earth, air, fire, and water.

Your weaving can reflect the birthdays or anniversaries of combinations of people in your family using birthstone colors to reflect the dates. Here is a sample of colors for a May wedding of two people born in February and August.

The graphic sun image of the Textile Traditions bag is inspired by an icon that is common in cultures that practice knotted cut pile.

images

Creating original images to weave in unique fabric can seem daunting, but it is just a step-by-step process. Start with an idea, a design, a photo, a memory; the process from concept to creation is the same. Work in series: start with one idea, and in the process of designing, weaving, and finishing that idea, others will come. Keep a sketchbook handy. Getting started is the hardest part—once you put pen to paper, you have an image to work with, whether you alter it, add to it, color it in, or keep it as is.

The most satisfying work is something you do from your own inspiration or memory, expressing your ideas or your history. We can use images from our own ancestral past or make up new images of our own. Your life is full of details that can be stored as images in your work. Express what is important in your life.

inspiration from tradition

There are cultures around the world that can define their world by a focused vocabulary of symbols and imagery. Traditional icons and shapes can be a rich source of ideas. Explore the images of cultures that are important to you, either by ancestry or affinity.

Textile inspirations abound. Carpet designs from Central Asia, ikat fabrics of Indonesia, India, Guatemala, and Japan are rich resources for textile-inspired designs. Kente cloth from West Africa or suzanis from Uzbekistan are rich with possibilities for knotted pile, as are bandweaving patterns and colors from Latvia, Estonia, and Lithuania, which can easily translate into a soumak or knotted pile border.

Designs and symbolism used in traditional textiles are rooted in the cultures that create them. Designs are handed down from weaver to weaver, changing with time, place, weaver, and materials. We may look at an image and wonder whether it has not varied at all over 5,000 years or is an invention of a very recent weaver.

Borders are traditional in knotted pile textiles and play an important part in the design process. They contain the view, narrow the viewer's focus, and surround and help define the graphic image. Sometimes borders invade or affect the central image; sometimes they are invaded by the image. Borders can be planned to complement the design narrative, or they can remain benign, like simple stripes. They can also present a separate story of their own.

personal inspiration

Even though weaving with folk techniques is rooted in tradition, we are not bound by that tradition. I have tried to make my work a bridge between the traditional and the contemporary, and I continue to develop and use a personal vocabulary of symbols. I use whichever design catches my eye and assign my own personal meaning to it, or even make up new images.

The Travel Bag pulls together three different design ideas with personal significance, each evoking a sense of place. The first cut pile pocket, Night Sky, is the view I had from an airplane window landing late at night in Detroit. The diagonal slash of street lights caught my eye as we came in to land, and it seemed an apt metaphor for traveling, cutting across the land and through time as we do. There were grids of golden lights that were parking lots and lines of lights that

appeared to bulge at intersections or shopping centers.

The other pocket pattern was a similar inspiration: this time, landing in Denver on a cold, snowy January afternoon. There was a golden late afternoon sun shining under cloud cover, turning the stubble field into a glowing rust, that contrasted with fallow fields of black soil. There were snow-covered fields with fences poking out and furrowed fields with snow

in the furrows. We often comment on the similarity of farmland to patchwork quilt patterns, so I adapted the colors and used a quilt motif.

The band for the travel bag was inspired by a student of mine who wove an inkle band of black warps with one yellow strand in the center, which looked like a road with a broken yellow center line. I expanded on the idea with a double yellow line down the center and a white line on each side, which evokes the fog lines at the edges of the road here in California. This is the road I travel every time I leave or come home.

You can use any number of design aids to help out at first: bead patterns, needlepoint graphs, cross-stitch patterns, and design books for other techniques like stranded knitting, stained glass, quilting, even children's coloring books. Ideas can come from textiles you like: rugs, bags, and home furnishings. Quilt blocks and woven coverlet designs are a rich source of designs. Sketch ideas from other design sources and translate them in to graphed patterns you can use for weaving. You don't have to copy, or use the whole design. A fragment, an impression, or colors may be enough to remind you and serve as your memento.

The view from my window on an airplane near Denver

building images

Isolate an idea or image and think of a motif that is representative of that idea. I live in the foothills, so I'll use a conifer—a simple tree that looks like a child's drawing—as my starting point to explore the possibilities of a simple image.

I can repeat this tree in a linear fashion for a border. Fill in the space between the trees to join them, adding a borderline to each side—now it becomes a reciprocating border, which is common to textiles from Central Asia. Create a turn for the corners.

Some designs need to fill more space. I could rotate the tree line for a larger border, then fill in and add borderlines and the corners. Experiment with the components for different variations.

You can work with your image; it does not have to be static. Instead of border designs, rotate the tree for a medallion. Fill the empty squares in between the images and add color. The tree is still present, but it is not a dominant image. The final design represents something particular to me, but it can be interpreted by a viewer in many ways, some of which have nothing to do with trees.

focus and editing

Decide what it is you are trying to convey. Is it an idea, a feeling, a place? Not every image needs to make it into every design. Break it down into parts, ideas, words, and see if you can narrow your choices and refine your design. Try making the images simple, graphic, understandable, and still effective in conveying the underlying idea. Take a few liberties with reality!

Complexity, with layers of borders and small images that fill in every available space in a design, can overpower an idea. Simplicity is a challenge: the need to focus the image and still maintain a pleasing graphic composition.

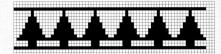

A tree is a simple beginning. Repeat the tree and add a borderline and join the trees for a reciprocating border.

Another tree forms a corner turn.

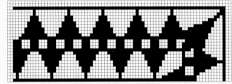

Rotate the trees for a wider border. Add borderlines and a corner turn, then connect elements.

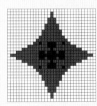

Color in the trees and add color between them for a patchwork motif.

Add more colors to fill out a square. The initial tree image is hard to see in the finished design.

choosing
embellishments

First Bag Series

Weaving is just the beginning of these bags. The cloth is the structure on which the construction depends, and it helps set the parameters for all of the decisions you make, but the details of construction really make the project unique and can make or break the finished bag. Each step in the process of construction should enhance the woven fabric and carry through your inspiration. It may be a color, a choice of beads or embellishments, or the graphic image that gives clues to the meaning therein.

Embellishment details are determined by the type and size of bag you are making. Each bag has its own construction methods, and you will find and develop construction methods of your own. The details are what will make the bag something uniquely yours, something that stands out. I usually don't plan embellishments until I have started weaving: some bags will need more punch; for some, the bag itself is enough. Bags that are already heavy with images usually need very little else. The pile bags often have less embellishment; they rely on the woven fabric to deliver the message.

Nathan Menz

The embellishment process is step by step for me—trial and error, a process of choices and elimination.

One of the bags in the First Bag series has an iridescent blue button.

I liked the color, but the button was overpowering by itself and seemed to stick out too much. The solution was to keep going—embellish further—to make the button look more at home. I started with some nailhead beads sewn along the edge of the leather binding. That helped some, but I still thought the button looked too big and out of scale. The answer was to add some embellishments more in scale with the button. After trying a variety of bead combinations in different orders, I decided to space more iridescent beads along the top edge.

The embellishments on the rust-colored First Bag include flattened copper coins. With their denomination and source obscured, they bring a sense of age. Paired with the camel button and set against the traditional-looking colors, the bag suggests distant lands.

There can be details that have meaning only to you, such as buttons from your family's button box. You can use fetishes that have symbolic or religious meaning to you, from the sublime to the ridiculous: bottle caps, coins, buttons, medallions, medals, or old jewelry. Whether you collect or make your own fetishes or have friends who make buttons or jewelry, embellishments can make the work of your hands unique.

Charlene Abrams

Oak Grove Studio

the
bag series

Following the first bag I made from the remnant of silk fabric, the series of woven bags and purses has led to explorations of weaving in a variety of directions. I have created bags based on puns, goddesses, traditional textiles, and song lyrics. The first few bags began as a word-association game using the term "bag." My first woven bag was the Coin Purse (shown on page 4), followed by Alligator Bag, Doggie Bag, and others.

Sandwich Bag: This whimsical design takes a literal look at the lunchbox staple. The embellishments of beaded lettuce and tomatoes are integral to this bag.

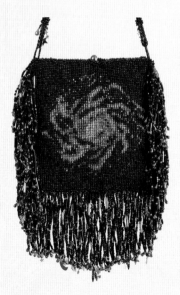

Evening Bag: The images I weave do not start out as a complete picture of the finished piece, but the sketch or graph begins the process. This bag shows a spiral galaxy.

Beach Bag: This beaded bag explores different scenes from the ocean, seen from the shore and the water. The embellishments—fish, a beach ball, sea life, fishing lures—tie the bag together.

One of my early bags was handspun silk fabric, embellished with pick-up trims and fetishes. I spent lots of time spinning, dyeing, and weaving the fabric and trims for this bag, but the fetishes are really the message. A bag such as this can be made with any fabric and any trim or bands, as long as one can find all the fetishes that are sewn on to it. It was disappointing to realize that the unique work that went into this bag—the actual fabric—was secondary to the embellishments.

So I decided to make my own embellishments to make the bags truly unique, and now I make as many of the embellishments as I can.

Hand Bag: *The unique hand-dyed and handwoven fabric and trims of this bag take a back seat to the purchased hand fetishes and embellishments.*

Venus Bag: *This handspun silk bag is in the same series as Hand Bag, but since I made the fetishes and embellishments, they are unique and a lot more fun. Most of the metal used here is copper, the metal associated with Venus.*

Midwife's (or Frida's) Bag: *There can be things about the bags that only you know about, some secrets or surprises. This bag is embellished with frogs, which are symbols of transformation and fertility; inside the bag is another frog.*

Astarte Bag: *Named for the Sumerian goddess of souls.*

Carpet Bag sketch: My first idea for a carpet bag depicted an entire carpet woven from beads, with the idea that half of the carpet would show on each side.

Using textiles as a design source, I thought of a "carpet bag" and developed a design for beadweaving that would be folded in half to make a bag. I showed the design to my friend Orlo "Duke" Duker, a carpet weaver, who told me that traditional bags would be woven as a complete pattern on each face, not folded as I had drawn. I reworked the graph to have a complete design on one side. This first carpet bag inspired a series of beaded carpet bags. Eventually, I had difficulty finding beads in the colors that I wanted for the image. One day, I realized that I could use yarn rather than beads for carpet bags, so I asked Duke to teach me knotted pile.

Carpet Bag: Learning that a traditional carpet bag would show a complete design on each face, I redesigned the graph and wove the first in the carpet bag series.

Celtic Carpet Bag: In illuminated manuscripts, a page entirely decorated with designs but with no words is called a carpet page, which inspired the design for the next carpet bag in the series.

Ikat Bag: *The original Coin Purse gave me the idea of using imagery based on the painted-warp fabrics I weave. Loom-woven beads portray a folded length of fabric with a surface design of color blocks.*

Without knowing it, that one simple request would change the work that I have done ever since. I have been using these rug techniques, weaving, researching, and developing my own vocabulary of symbols, on a textile exploration that continues to unfold.

I hope to inspire a similar path for you.

Dancing Together: *The image of people dancing on the earth and stars dancing in the sky was inspired by a song lyric from the group Cielo y Terra (Heaven and Earth). I wove it first as a beaded carpet bag. After learning to weave cut pile, I wove it again in silk for a bag that I carry with me every day.*

resources

yarns

Brown Sheep Company Inc.
100662 Cty. Rd. 16
Mitchell, NE 69357
brownsheep.com
(800) 826-9136
Lamb's Pride

DMC Creative World
77 S. Hackensack Ave., Bldg. 10F
South Kearny, NJ 07032-4688
dmc-usa.com
(973) 589-0606
DMC Cotton

JCA Inc.
35 Scales Ln.
Townsend, MA 01469
jcacrafts.com
(978) 597-8794
Paternayan Persian Yarn

Norsk Fjord Fiber
PO Box 219
Sapphire, NC 28774
norskfjordfiber.com
(828) 884-2195
Vevgarn

Old Mill Yarn
109 E. Elizabeth
Eaton Rapids, MI 48827
oldmillyarn.com
(517) 663-2711
Davidson's Navaho Warp

Tahki Stacy Charles
70–30 80th St., Bldg 36
Ridgewood, NY 11385
tahkistacycharles.com
(800) 338-9276
Tahki Cotton Classic

tools

Ashford
Distributed in the United States by
Foxglove Fiberarts Supply
8040 NE Day Rd. W., Ste. 4F
Bainbridge Island, WA 98110
(206) 780-2747
foxglovefiber.com
Ashford rigid-heddle loom

Schacht Spindle Co.
6101 Ben Pl.
Boulder, CO 80301
schachtspindle.com
(303) 442-3212
Cricket loom
Flip loom

The publisher gratefully acknowledges Schacht Spindle Co. for the loan of tools used in photography for this book.

further reading

Chandler, Deborah. *Learning to Weave*. Loveland, Colorado: Interweave, 1995.

Collingwood, Peter. *Techniques of Rug Weaving*. New York: Watson Guptill, 1969. (Out of print.)

Crockett, Candace. *Card Weaving*. Loveland, Colorado: Interweave, 1991.

Davenport, Betty Lynn. *Hands On Rigid Heddle Weaving*. Loveland, Colorado: Interweave, 1987.

Mallett, Marla. *Woven Structures: A Guide to Oriental Rug and Textile Analysis*. Atlanta, Georgia: Christopher Publications, 1998.

Patrick, Jane. *Time to Weave: Simply Elegant Projects to Make in Almost No Time*. Loveland, Colorado: Interweave, 2006.

Wilson, Jean. *Jean Wilson's Soumak Workbook*. Loveland, Colorado: Interweave, 1982. (Out of print.)

———. *Pile Weaves: Twenty-Six Techniques and How to Do Them*. New York: Van Nostrand Reinhold, 1974. (Out of print.)

index